Bones in the Well

Bones in the Well

The Haun's Mill Massacre, 1838
A documentary history

by
Beth Shumway Moore

with a foreword by
Will Bagley

UNIVERSITY OF OKLAHOMA PRESS
Norman

Library of Congress Catalog Card Number 2006027638

Library of Congress Cataloging-in-Publication Data
Moore, Beth S. (Beth Shumway), 1927–
  Bones in the well : the Haun's Mill Massacre, 1838 : a documentary
history / by Beth S. Moore.
     p. cm.
  Includes bibliographical references and index.
  ISBN 978-0-8061-4270-8 (paper)
  1. Haun's Mill Massacre, Mo., 1838—Sources. 2. Mormons—Missouri—
History—19th century—Sources. 3. Mormons—Missouri—Biography.
4. Mormons—Crimes against—Missouri—History—19th century—
Sources. 5. Massacres—Missouri—Caldwell County—History—19th
century—Sources. 6. Missouri—Militia—History—19th century—
Sources. 7. Caldwell County (Mo.)—History—19th century—Sources.
8. Missouri—History —19th century—Sources. I. Title.

  F475.M8M66 2006
  977.8'03—dc22
                        2006027638

The paper in this book meets the guidelines for permanence and durability
of the Committee on Production Guidelines for Book Longevity of the
Council on Library Resources. ∞

Originally published in hardcover by the Arthur H. Clark Company,
copyright © 2006 by Beth Shumway Moore. Paperback edition published
2012 by the University of Oklahoma Press, Norman, Publishing Division
of the University. Manufactured in the U.S.A.

Contents

Foreword

Ever since British colonists began flooding through
Cumberland Gap in the 1770s, the American West
has been a violent and often brutal frontier. Kentucky could not have spawned a more aggressive generation
of men if Cadmus of Greek mythology had sown its dark
and bloody ground with dragon's teeth, and their descendents became a fierce pioneer people who settled much of
Tennessee, Missouri, and Arkansas. They left behind the
British tradition of "duty of retreat" in the face of aggression and replaced it with requiring that a man stand his
ground, coming to believe that while no hogs may need
stealing, there were plenty of bad men who needed killing.

It has recently become fashionable to argue that the
American frontier was not that violent, but this argument
is hard to sustain. The murder rate on overland emigrant
roads between 1840 and 1860 alone was twice today's national average, and violence in nineteenth-century America was
not limited to the frontier. Our history is full of dimly
remembered blood feuds, riots, and forgotten massacres.
Who recalls the Know-Nothing mobs in Philadelphia and
the repeated anti-Catholic riots in 1844 that led to the burning of the churches of St. Augustine and St. Michael and
the deaths of thirteen people? Ned Buntline inflamed the
same nativist sentiments to spark the Astor Place Riot in
May 1849, where ten or fifteen thousand New York fans of

actor Edwin Forrest rioted to protest an appearance in *Macbeth* by British aristocrat William Macready, killing some twenty-two people and injuring scores more. (Buntline served a year in prison for inciting the riot.)

A short list of Civil War atrocities—the massacres at Lawrence, Kansas; St. Louis, Centralia, Concordia, and Palmyra, Missouri; Poison Springs, Arkansas; Fort Pillow, Tennessee; Saltville, Virginia; and Hot Springs, North Carolina—recalls a level of savagry remarkable even in America's bloodiest war. The racial massacres at Elaine, Arkansas, in 1919 and at Tulsa, Oklahoma, in 1921—the latter, with its death toll of as many as two and three hundred people, may have been the worst act of terrorism in peacetime America until September 11, 2001—happened less than a century ago, but like the twenty other race riots Richard Hofstadter identified in which white aggressors massacred black victims, they have conveniently slipped from our national consciousness.

The murder of seventeen men and boys at a Missouri settlement known as Haun's Mill in 1838 is all but forgotten except by Latter-day Saints, better known as Mormons. Like other senseless acts of violence in our history, it should not be. Astonishingly, in the 168 years since it happened, no one has written a book about the Haun's Mill massacre, by far the most violent action ever taken against the Latter-day Saints. At last, a talented writer and historian has taken up this challenge. No one could be better suited for the task than Beth Moore, whose ancestors include some of the most celebrated and remarkable of Utah's pioneers, including Charles Shumway, who ferried the first families across the Mississippi during the evacuation of Nauvoo and who came to Utah in 1847 with Brigham Young.

No one can justify what happened at Haun's Mill. Juanita Brooks, a great and courageous historian, once spoke to a crowd composed largely of the children and grandchildren of people her grandfather had helped to kill at Mountain Meadows in southern Utah in 1857. She told them, "Nobody can forgive murder," but her life's work encouraged understanding a terrible atrocity and a level of compassion for the men whose lives were forever haunted by what they did one afternoon in a remote valley in the Great Basin.

Although I never had the privilege of meeting the remarkable Mrs. Brooks, I have had the honor of becoming a close friend with her spiritual successor, Beth Moore, whose life and background share many similarities with the most courageous historian Mormonism ever produced. Like Juanita Brooks, Beth was born on one of the ragged edges of the Mormon frontier, the Bighorn Basin of Wyoming, where she came of age during the Great Depression. Both are descendants of men who were at Mountain Meadows on that fateful September day in 1857, and Beth's great-grandfather, Nephi Johnson, inspired the woman he called "the little schoolteacher" to tell the truth about that sad and terrible event. Both Brooks and Moore devoted their professional lives to teaching in a culture that rewards salesmen much more generously than it does those to whom it entrusts the future of its children. And both women have told stories no one else cared to tell.

More than most documentary histories, *Bones in the Well* serves up large chunks of history—raw. No journalist wrote a contemporary account of the slaughter on Shoal Creek, but this work collects the eyewitness affidavits (many taken not long after it happened), later newspaper articles, and recollections of the event, and uses early historical accounts to help put the atrocity in context. These survivors' stories are filled with harrowing imagery. Amanda Smith recalled how the scent of blood terrified even the cattle; John Hammer described seeing a crimson vapor rising from the mill site "like a transparent pillar of blood" as his father was killed. They make the horror and distress immediate and visceral: you can smell the blood that gathered in pools on the black-smith shop's killing floor, and hear the groaning of the wounded, the bellowing cattle, the howling dogs, the piercing cries of the fatherless, "and from the black woods the dismal hooting of owls."

The Missouri ruffians "burned all the books that they could find, they shot the hogs and cattle, it seemed for pleasure of shooting game, as they did not consume near all they killed," David Lewis recalled. The actions of "this band of murderers"—particularly the killing of children and the execution of the Mormon wounded, the desecration of Thomas McBride's corpse, the "plundering the pockets of the dead striping off their boots, shoes, and clothing," and the looting of the settlement—suggest such criminals would be little bothered by their acts, but time and conscience work on all but the most depraved. The year after the massacre, the *Peoria Register* pondered this "dark and bloody page" in the annals of Missouri and concluded her future citizens would look upon the killings with shame and horror, "and the perpetrators of these atrocities, if not divested of all the attributes of men, will be haunted to their dying day by remorse more terrible than the tearing of the vulture at the heart of the fabled Prometheus." Not one of the Missouri militiamen ever described what happened that autumn day: perhaps they found it too terrible to remember, just as the murders were impossible to justify.

Bones in the Well includes massacre survivor Willard G. Smith's story of how he met one of the killers of his father and brother while serving in the Mormon Battalion, a tradition that also survives among the descendants of another massacre victim, Austin Hammer. They recall that his son, John, craved vengeance so much he felt he would "crawl on ice and snow for a mile to get a shot at one of that Haun's Mill mob." While pitching a tent in a military camp outside Carson City many years later, a stranger asked his company's captain if any of his men had relatives killed at Haun's Mill, and the officer pointed out the son, John Hammer. The man confessed he had participated in the savagery at Haun's Mill. Hammer suppressed the urge to drive the axe he had in his hand into the man's head. "The Lord let him see into the very inner parts of the stranger's soul," the story goes, and words could not describe the man's misery. "I hear their groans all day long. I have no rest day or night and I see their forms all night," the stranger confessed, and he asked Hammer to kill him, but Hammer sent the wretch on his way. He lost his desire for revenge, "for he felt that the Lord was doing a much better job of it."

As the daily news brings reports of genocide in the Congo, Rwanda, Darfur, and Sudan on a scale unimaginable to earlier generations, the bones in the well at the site of the Haun's Mill massacre teach us much and give us even more to ponder about fear, hatred, and religion. Let us hope they show the futility of vengeance and give us hope that there is justice and mercy in the eternities.

WILL BAGLEY
August 2006

Acknowledgments

My sincere thanks go out to the following individuals who helped with this project:

- Will Bagley took the time from his busy schedule to answer many questions, provide background data, and help me find source references. His aid has been extremely valuable in producing this book.

- Robert A. Clark of the Arthur H. Clark Company spent time answering my many questions about preparing a manuscript for press, in editing and source-checking, and gave encouragement in completing the project.

- Gale and Marilyn Lindstrom contributed valuable comments and critiqued the book in its infancy.

- Cousin Jayne Knowleton Brewer spent hours in the BYU library to aid in my research.

- Blackhawk and Mason Walters added their suggestions and contributed the title: *Bones in the Well*.

- My writer's group, WIG, of St. George, Utah, provided valuable critiques.

- My Family Home Evening group, Apple Valley Home Evening Group, spent an evening offering suggestions.

- My friend Marilyn Richardson contributed a copy of the journal of her great-grandfather, Isaac Laney, about the Haun's Mill massacre.

- My daughter-in-law Kathie Workman Moore contributed a copy of the journal of David Lewis, her great-great-grandfather, about the Haun's Mill massacre.

- Einar Erickson's interest in my efforts and ability to answer questions have been deeply appreciated.

- And to the many I haven't mentioned who have shown interest in my efforts, thank you.

Prologue

Meanwhile was being matured the bloody tragedy which occurred on the 30th of October, near Haun's Mill, on Shoal Creek, about twenty miles below Far West. Besides the Mormons living there were a number of emigrants awaiting the cessation of hostilities before proceeding on their journey. It had been agreed between the Mormons and Missourians of that locality that they would not molest each other, but live together in peace. But the men of Caldwell and Daviess Counties would not have it so. Suddenly and without warning, on the day above-mentioned, mounted and to the number of two hundred and forty, they fell upon the fated settlement. While the men were at their work out of doors, the women in the house, and the children playing about the yards, the crack of a hundred rifles was heard, and before the firing ceased eighteen of these unoffending people were stretched dead upon the ground, while many more were wounded. I will not enter upon the sickening details, which are copious and fully proven; suffice it to say that never in savage or other warfare was there perpetrated an act more dastardly and brutal. Indeed, it was openly avowed by the men of Missouri that it was no worse to shoot a Mormon than to shoot an Indian, and killing Indians was no worse than killing wild beasts.

—H. H. Bancroft, *History of Utah*, 128.

This tale is but a small part of the history of the Church of Jesus Christ of Latter-day Saints (LDS). The little-known event that occurred on October 30, 1838, at Haun's Mill, Missouri, is perhaps only a footnote in that larger story, but it looms large in the tumultuous events that shaped the attitudes and beliefs of the nine-teenth-century adherents called Mormons, who followed the teachings and revelations of their prophet, Joseph Smith

The United States of America is a land where the free-dom to practice one's religion is historically honored. But in the nineteenth century this was not true for the Mormons. In the face of armed assault and banishment from Missouri, church leaders appealed to President Van Buren for help. His response, as given in *History of the Church*, was, "What can I do? I can do nothing for you. If I do anything I shall come in contact with the whole state of Missouri."[1] Gover-nor L. W. Boggs of Missouri had issued an order on Octo-ber 27, 1838, declaring that Mormons had to either leave the state or they would be killed. Known as the Extermination Order, it stated, in part:

> I have received by Amos Reese, Esq., of Ray county, and Wiley C. Williams, Esq., one of my aids, information of the most appalling character, which entirely changes the face of things, and places the Mormons in the attitude of an open and avowed defiance of the laws, and of having made war upon the people of this state. Your orders are, therefore, to hasten your operation with all possible speed. The Mormons must be treated as ene-mies, and must be exterminated or driven from the state if nec-essary for the public peace—their outrages are beyond all description.

Not until July 4, 1976, was this proclamation formally removed, with a heartfelt apology from the state of Missouri.

In less than a decade the Mormons would be driven once again from their homes in and around their city of Nauvoo, Illinois; their prophet killed while in jail; and their city dev-astated. It wasn't until March 2004 that the state of Illinois printed an apology to the Mormons for the injustices done

---

[1]Smith Jr., *History of the Church*, vol. 4, 40.

to them in their state in the 1830s and 1840s. The well-known Mormon critic J. B. Turner stated in the early 1840s:

> Who began the quarrel? Was it the Mormons? Is it not notori-
> ous, on the contrary, that they were hunted, like wild beasts,
> from county to county, before they made any desperate resist-
> ance? Did they ever, as a body, refuse obedience to the laws,
> when called upon to do so, until driven to desperation by repeat-
> ed threats and assaults on the part of the mob? Did the state ever
> make one decent effort to defend them, as fellow-citizens, in
> their rights, or to redress their wrongs? Let the conduct of its
> governors, attorneys, and the fate of their final petitions answer.
> Have any who plundered and openly massacred the Mormons
> ever been brought to the punishment due to their crimes? Let
> the boasting murderers of begging and helpless infancy answer.
> Has the state ever remunerated even those known to be inno-
> cent, for the loss of either their property or their arms? Did either
> the pulpit or the press through the state raise a note of remon-
> strance or alarm? Let the clergymen who abetted, and the edi-
> tors who encouraged the mob, answer. We know that there were
> many noble exceptions, but, alas, that they were so few! We hate
> the Mormons imposture, it is from beginning to end utterly
> detestable, both in its principles and its effects.[2]

Why were the Mormons so reviled? There were many reasons that non-Mormons found them intolerable. They had their own stores and economic system. They were clan-nish and voted in a bloc, thus tipping elections in their favor. They had a "different" religion and considered their faith superior to all others. They were friendly to the Indians and thought to be abolitionists. Missouri was a slave state, and the western portion, where the Mormons settled, was also home to a great number of emigrants from the South. Many of the Mormon settlers in Missouri were from New Eng-land, bringing with them a regional bias against slavery. Additionally, the Mormons invited blacks to join their

---

[2]Turner, *Mormonism in All Ages,* 57.

church, something almost unheard of in slave states at that time. To the slave-holding Missourians, the Mormons were on the wrong side of the slavery issue, whether or not they were abolitionists. But none of these idiosyncracies justified the violence and hostility visited upon them.

Two thousand years ago, when the early Christians were enduring terrible persecutions, Gamaliel, a Pharisee and doctor of the law, said, "And now I say unto you, Refrain from these men, and let them alone: for if this counsel or this work be of men, it will come to nought: But if it be of God, ye cannot overthrow it; lest haply ye be found even to fight against God."[3]

A nation needs to know its history so that, hopefully, its wrongs will not be repeated. The story of the Haun's Mill massacre bears retelling for just that reason.

---

[3] Acts 5: 38–39.

Introduction

The families gathered at Haun's Mill were unaware that danger lurked on the horizon that autumn day of October 30, 1838. After all, hadn't one of their own met with the militia of the surrounding area only a few days before? Both sides had agreed on peace, a peace that was not to be.

Escalating conflict between the Missourians and members of the Church of Jesus Christ of Latter-day Saints, known as Mormons, had created a state of near-panic in the population of northwest Missouri. In response to the urging of their founder and prophet Joseph Smith, Mormons from far and wide were gathering at Far West in hopes of protection and safety from non-Mormon militia forces and other marauding groups who were harassing the Saints.

Jacob Haun, after whom the small settlement on Shoal Creek in Caldwell County had been named, traveled to Far West to meet the prophet. It was reported later that Joseph Smith advised Haun to bring those who had settled around his mill to Far West and join the larger group of Mormons in that settlement. "You had better lose your property than your lives," Smith reportedly told him. Haun was adamant that he could maintain his holdings, so he did not move to Far West. After he left, Smith told others, "I wish they were here for their own safety. I am confident they will be butchered in the most fearful manner." Unfortunately, the prophecy came true.

The landscape surrounding Haun's Mill was dotted with a few cabins, along with wagon boxes and tents. Approximately twenty-five families had settled there in the past two years, but the population had swelled recently as a few groups traveling from Ohio and other points east stopped on their way to Far West, following their prophet's call.

Smoke carried the smell of cook fires skyward, creating a haze through which a bright orange sun shone. A breeze sent the few remaining leaves on the branches to join those on the ground. In the nearby meadows, horses and cows grazed.

Children crunched through the leaves, scattering them and burying themselves as they laughed and called to each other. Their happy voices sounded like music accompanied by the pounding of the hammer and anvil and the swish of the mill wheel. Some gathered nuts or splashed and played in Shoal Creek or the mill pond. It was quite a warm day for October. Older siblings watched toddlers and tended babies while their mothers gathered clothes off the line or prepared supper. Some men worked to finish the blacksmith shop, while others, along with older children, worked in the fields, gathering wheat, shucking dry corn stalks, gleaning potatoes, carrots, and onions that had been missed. All rejoiced in the abundant harvest intended to provide their winter food.

The murmur of voices, an occasional song, and the soothing sound of the creek made an Arcadian atmosphere.

Suddenly the peace was shattered by about two hundred horses pounding the earth and sending chunks of dirt and sod flying upward from the thundering hooves. Strange men crouched low, urging their horses onward. Their yells filled the air with chilling savagery. The Livingston County militia, led by Colonel Thomas Jennings, formed in three square positions with a vanguard, covering all sides except the slowly moving stream on the south. Every man, woman, and child froze like a still-life painting for long minutes.

Nehemiah Comstock fired a gun in the air, waited ten seconds, and attacked the settlement. Screams and cries of "peace, quarter, and mercy" were wasted.

When they finished killing all those who were accessible, the mob turned to looting and destroying crops and the gathered winter food, in addition to livestock.

At twilight the marauders finally left and the survivors ventured forth, tending to the wounded the best they could, and crying over the dead—seventeen had been killed and several wounded severely, two of whom would later die of their wounds. In the morning, after a restless night dominated by fear that the mob would return, they slid their dead into a newly half-dug well, shoveling dirt over them.

The militia returned the next day under the command of Colonel Jennings. The Mormon men who hadn't been killed or wounded were hiding, so it was easy to further loot the small community, leaving the people destitute.

❀   ❀   ❀

Haun's Mill was a natural stopping place for Mormons migrating from Kirtland, Ohio, where many of the Saints lived. It was located in Caldwell County, which was formed on December 26, 1836, out of Ray County by the Missouri legislature as a place for the Mormons, assuming that they would not occupy Ray, Clay, and other Missouri counties.

The small settlement had been founded sometime in the mid-1830s by Jacob Haun, a recent convert to the Church of Jesus Christ of Latter-day Saints, and a mill was constructed there on Shoal Creek.[1] Haun was an inventive,

---

[1] Haun was born January 13, 1804, in Ontario County, New York. He married Harriet Elizabeth Pearson in November 1833 in Newark, New Jersey, and they converted to the Mormon church and emigrated to Missouri. He and his family emigrated to Oregon in 1843, where he died in 1860. Following the massacre his name does not appear in the records of the LDS church. McMinnville, Oregon, *News Register*, March 8, 2005. See also Ralph C. Geer, "Occasional Address for the Year 1847," *Transactions of the Ninth Annual Reunion of the Oregon Pioneer Association*, 1879.

competent builder and miller, and soon others began to gather at the site of his mill.

The people in this sparsely settled section of northwest Missouri who had welcomed the Mormons earned the name of "Jack Mormons" from the resentful residents of Clay and Jackson.[2] Peace was maintained for about three years from the time the Mormons left Jackson County. But as the Mormon population increased, the "old settlers" who had once welcomed them changed their attitude, having no inclination to become the minority.

Unfortunately many Mormons lacked tact, and claimed their church intended to possess the land—that they were the "chosen people" with the only "true church." Many of their leaders counseled the Saints to be discreet and live their religion, which the majority did; however rumors, often unfounded, were enlarged upon, increasing with every telling. Consequently the original landowners felt threatened and were easily stirred up by lawless and angry men, some of them former members of the Mormon church who roamed the frontier looking for excitement and trouble.

Relations between church members and the Missouri citizens deteriorated further following the arrival of Joseph Smith and other church leaders from Ohio in 1838. Livingston County called out its militia and two companies patrolled, turning back migrants from Ohio and guarding the borders adjoining Caldwell County.

Trouble accelerated with an election incident at Gallatin, Missouri, on August 6, 1838. Local citizens objected to the Mormons' voting. This led to angry words escalating into a brawl. No one was killed, but several were injured.

---

[2] "Because of their friendliness toward the beleagured Saints, the helpful citizens of Clay and other counties were criticized by hostile elements in Jackson County and dubbed 'Jack Mormons,' a term applied widely in the nineteenth century to friendly non-Mormons." Allen and Leonard, *The Story of the Latter-day Saints*, 98.

The counties in northwestern Missouri were in a virtual state of civil war.

> In the civil strife neighboring counties behaved like sovereign states, conducting border warfare and threatening invasion and counter invasion. The Missourians meant to drive the Mormon "from Daviess to Caldwell, and from Caldwell to hell," and the Mormons were equally determined to "make clean work now and expel the mob from Daviess and then from Caldwell." One inflammatory incident led to another. Rumor and exaggeration ran riot, defense was often mistaken for aggression, and fear and hatred decided each new blow. With both Missourians and Mormons taking the law into their own hands, mob and militia became indistinguishable, and Governor Lilburn W. Boggs himself declared: "The quarrel is between the Mormons and the mob, and they can fight it out." Both sides had become too desperate to listen to reason.[3]

Governor Boggs faced increasing pressure to act, as both Mormons and non-Mormons petitioned him to act in their defense. The militia in the counties surrounding Caldwell County quickly swelled to hundreds, and in the days preceding the massacre, word reached the Mormons at Haun's Mill about the events in Daviess County and at Crooked River, just south of Caldwell County.

The Battle of Crooked River is credited by many historians as having a direct influence on the infamous Extermination Order subsequently issued by Governor Boggs and on events at Haun's Mill. There is no doubt that the countryside was further inflamed by the event.

During the first part of October 1838 several hundred Latter-day Saints from De Witt, Carroll County, were forcibly removed from their homes. It was not the first time Mormons had been forced from their homes and lands in the state. Following the dislocation of the De Witt Saints, Mis-

[3]Mulder and Mortensen, *Among the Mormons*, 98.

souri assailants continued to threaten Mormons in Daviess County. Mormons responded with retaliatory aggression.

Rumors flew: the Mormons were going to invade Ray County, south of Caldwell County; the residents appealed to Governor Boggs for help. The commander of the state militia in northwestern Missouri ordered Captain Samuel Bogart of Clay County to patrol the no man's land below the county line, known as "Bunkham's Strip" or "Buncombe Strip," to block Mormon entry into Ray County. Bogart, an anti-Mormon Methodist preacher who had previously participated in a vigilante group that harried the Mormons in Carroll County, began to patrol the county line. Word spread of Bogart harassing Mormons and capturing three prisoners.

Exaggerated reports quickly reached Far West, to the effect that a "mob" had captured and intended to execute the prisoners. The Mormons immediately mustered their forces. In the fight that followed, the Mormons attacked and broke the militia's lines. The Missourians fled in all directions. One militiaman and three Mormons were killed in the encounter. The three prisoners were rescued. The Mormons collected their wounded and made their way back to Far West.[4]

Although the battle resulted in only four fatalities, the effect was a massive escalation of the civil conflict. After receiving hysterical reports from Missouri citizens and, it would appear, refusing to listen to the Mormons, Governor Boggs charged the Latter-day Saints with open rebellion, called out 2,500 state militiamen, and issued his Extermination Order on October 27, 1838: "The Mormons must be treated as enemies, and must be exterminated or driven from the State if necessary for the public peace—their outrages are beyond all description."[5]

---

[4]LeSueur, *The 1838 Mormon War in Missouri,* 141–42. See also Baugh, *A Call to Arms,* for a summary of this event.

[5]The role that Governor Boggs' order played in the massacre at Haun's Mill has long been debated. Alexander Baugh offers a clear timeline and explanation of the

The governor's use of the word *exterminate* may have been intentionally based on its prior use by the Mormons earlier in 1838. Sidney Rigdon, first counselor to Joseph Smith and a superb orator, gave a speech on July 4, 1838, that included the following phrase: "And the mob that comes on us to disturb us, it shall be between us and them a war of extermination, for we will follow them till the last drop of blood is spilled, or else they will have to exterminate us."[6]

Strangely, the iron fist that Boggs so quickly ungloved was in direct contrast to his passive attitude during the five years the Mormons were being battered from pillar to post by the Missourians. With the Saints now on the offensive, Boggs donned the cloak of public protector—his intense dislike for all things Mormon had not dimmed since the early days in Jackson County.

❀   ❀   ❀

Up to this point the people at Haun's Mill had lived in peace with their neighbors, but they now organized a group of about thirty men armed with shotguns and squirrel rifles. David Evans was chosen as captain.[7] Through a messenger he entered into a truce on October 28 with Captain Nehemiah Comstock, the leader of the militia in the local area.[8]

---

sequence of events surrounding this debate. It is his contention that word of the Extermination Order did not reach either the Mormons at Far West or the Missourians who attacked the settlement at Haun's Mill until the day after the massacre. See Baugh, *A Call to Arms,* 127.

[6]Harold Schindler, in his biography of Orrin Porter Rockwell, compares the use of the word *exterminate* by Rigdon and Boggs, 49–50.

[7]David Evans (1804–1883) was both a spiritual and military leader of the group in Haun's Mill. He moved to Far West, later to Nauvoo, and crossed the plains to Salt Lake City, arriving on September 15, 1850. He remained a prominent leader in church and civic affairs.

[8]At least four meetings were held to try and negotiate a truce. David Evans, Jacob Myers Sr., and Anthony Blackburn met at Myers's settlement. Evans also negotiated a truce via messenger with another group from Livingston County. In addition, at least two meetings were held at the home of Oliver Walker. For details, see Baugh, *A Call to Arms,* 117.

Both groups agreed to disarm their military organizations, and Captain Comstock agreed that as long as the Mormons were law-abiding, they would live in peace. But word came to Haun's Mill that another company under Captain William Mann was marching toward them. The Mormons evidently trusted Captain Comstock because he had been friendly and cooperative with them, but not Captain Mann. As will be related by Burr Joyce later in this book, Mann had been turning Mormons emigrants back on their way to Caldwell County, taking their guns, and harassing them in other ways. So the night patrols of the Mormons at Haun's Mill were resumed. When Comstock heard that the Mormons had not disarmed, he yielded to the pressures of his men and prepared to lead the unexpected attack with help from Captain Thomas R. Bryan, William Mann, and Colonel William O. Jennings, sheriff of Livingston County.

And so the stage was set for the massacre. And the echoes of the tragedy that occurred in that bucolic setting still ring. Who better to tell the tale than those who were there? Their stories, preserved in journals and reminiscences, have survived through the years. The gathering of these accounts gives immediacy to the recounting of the tragedy. May their voices serve as a reminder of the cruelty we too often visit on one another in the hope that we may, one day, find tolerance and compassion.

The accounts that follow are unedited, without correction of spelling or punctuation. The author's introductions to the sources are typeset in italics to differentiate them from the original documents.

I

Most Cruel Deed—1838

For the context and background of the eyewitness accounts
that make up this book, few sources provide as objective a
telling of this harrowing event than the one Burr Joyce composed fifty years after it took place.[1] In the chapters that follow, many
of these accounts and a few contemporary newspaper reports will
also be reprinted. As the various accounts unfold, there will be rep-
etitions, of course, especially involving the tale of the two murdered
boys and Mr. McBride, who was badly mutilated by his murderer. Each writer offers a different viewpoint, and often new facts.
And always there is deep emotion portrayed.

In his paper on the massacre, Alma R. Blair states that the
difficulty of reconstructing the event is twofold. The first challenge
is determining the facts—how many persons were at the mill, how
large was the attacking force, and exactly what happened. The second challenge is the fact that the accounts of the Mormons relate
more of the horror and the atrocities committed than actual facts.[2]

The following article was written by Burr Joyce—a pen name for
Major Return S. Holcombe, a prolific writer and author of one of
the best of the Missouri county histories. Historian Harold Schindler
considers this the best single account of the massacre.[3]

Holcombe is unable to provide reasons for the attack. It is not
known if he was a Mormon, but he refers to the prophet Joseph as Joe
Smith and several times as simply Smith, titles that Smith's fol-

---

[1] Smith III, *The History of the Reorganized Church*, vol. 2, 224–32. The Reorganized
Church of Jesus Christ of Latter Day Saints is now called the Community of
Christ.

[2] Blair, "The Haun's Mill Massacre," BYU Studies 13 (Autumn 1972): 62–67.

[3] Schindler, *Orrin Porter Rockwell*, 51.

lowers would never have used. Yet he refers to the militia and mob as Gentiles, a term used by the Mormons for non-Mormons. Whatever his faith, he attempted to write an objective account of what happened. His article was printed in the two newspapers cited in the text and copied into the Reorganized Church of Jesus Christ of Latter Day Saints (Community of Christ) history.

❋ ❋ ❋

In this chapter we record one of the most cruel deeds of blood known to the history of the age. We would gladly draw the curtain and say nothing regarding this horrible affair, but we have no right to cover up or conceal the facts of history. Nor can we resist the conclusion that this butchery was the direct and legitimate result of the exterminating order of the chief executive of the State of Missouri. By this were these desperate, cruel, and blood thirsty men impelled to this deed that causes humanity to blush. The horrible consequences of this awful deed must by the faithful historian be laid at the door of Governor Lilburn W. Boggs.

We might compile an account of this from church records, but we prefer to present it to our readers from the pens of men who were not connected with it, and who dispassionately viewed the matter after years had dispelled the intense feeling of the time.

The following is the account as written by Burr Joyce, and published in the *St. Louis Globe-Democrat* for October 6, 1887, and reproduced in the *Saints' Herald* for October 22, 1887:

THE HAUN'S MILL MASSACRE
AN INCIDENT OF THE MORMON WAR IN MISSOURI

Special Correspondence of the Globe-Democrat
Breckenridge, Missouri, September 27, 1887
In the afternoon of Tuesday, October 30, 1838, during the Mormon war in Missouri, there occurred in Caldwell Coun-

ty a dreadful incident, generally termed "The Haun's Mill Massacre." From official documents and other records, from affidavits of witnesses, and from statements made by actual participants, I have prepared the following account. If any newspaper publication of the affair has ever before been made, I am not aware of the fact.

The Mormons made their first settlement in Missouri, in Jackson County, in the year 1832, under the leadership of their "prophet," Joseph Smith. I have not the space here to describe their experiences in that county, their expulsion therefrom, their sojourn in Clay and Ray, the "treaty" by which they were given Caldwell County as a sort of reservation, the founding of the city of Far West, nor can I narrate the circumstances leading to the Mormon war (so called), and finally the banishment of these unhappy people from the State. All these incidents may form the subject of a future paper. I may state, however, that the massacre was perpetrated on the very day that the militia, under Generals Lucas and Doniphan, arrived at Far West, with orders from Governor Boggs to "expel the Mormons from the State or exterminate them."

At Jacob Haun's mill, on Shoal Creek, in the eastern part of Caldwell County, about eight miles south of Breckenridge, there had collected about twenty Mormon families. Haun himself was a Mormon and had come to the site from Wisconsin a few years before. He had a very good mill, and clustered around it were a blacksmith shop and half a dozen small houses. The alarm that the troops were moving against them had driven nearly all the Mormon families in the county to Far West for safety. A dozen or more living in the vicinity repaired to Haun's mill, which was twenty miles to the eastward of Far West. As there were not enough houses to accommodate all of the fugitives, a number were living in tents and temporary shelters. A few families, perhaps four, had come in on the evening of the 29th, from Ohio, and were occupying their emigrants' wagons. Not one member of the little community had ever been in arms against the "Gentiles," or taken any part whatever in the preceding disturbances.

Word that the militia of the State had been ordered to expel them from the country had reached the Mormons of the Haun's mill settlement, and following this intelligence came a report that a considerable number of men in Livingston County, together with some from Daviess, had organized in the forks of Grand River, near Spring Hill, in Livingston, and were preparing to attack them. Whereupon a company of about twenty-five men and boys, indifferently armed with shotguns and squirrel rifles, was organized at the mill, and David Evans was chosen captain. It was resolved to defend the place against the threatened assault. Some of the older men urged that on Crooked River (October 25) Haun himself went to Far West to take counsel of Joe Smith. "Move here, by all means, if you wish to save your lives," said the prophet. Haun replied that if the settlers should abandon their homes, the Gentiles would burn their houses and other buildings and destroy all of the property left behind. "Better lose your property than your lives," rejoined Smith. Haun represented that he and his neighbors were willing to defend themselves against what he called "the mob," and Smith finally gave them permission to remain. Others at the mill opposed a retreat, and when an old man named Myers reminded them how few they were, and how many the "Gentiles" numbers, they declared that the Almighty would send his angels to their help when the day of the battle should come. Some of the women, too, urged the men to stand firm, and offered to mold bullets and prepare patching for the rifles if necessary.

North of the mill was a body of timber half a mile in width, skirting Shoal Creek; beyond was a stretch of prairie. For a day or two Capt. Evans kept a picket post in the northern border of the timber, but on the 28th he entered into a sort of truce with Capt. Nehemiah Comstock, commanding a company of Livingston "Gentiles" from the settlements near Mooresville and Utica, and the post was withdrawn. By the terms of this truce, which was effected by a messenger who rode between Evans and Comstock, the Gentiles were to let the Mormons alone as long as the latter were peaceable, and vice versa. Each party, too, was to disband its military organization. But on the morning of the 29th the Mormons learned that a company of Livingston militia, a few miles to the eastward, were menacing them, and so they maintained their organization and that night set watches. The latter company was commanded by Captain William Mann, and for some days had been operating at and in the vicinity of Whitney's mill, on Lower Shoal Creek (where the village of Dawn now stands), stopping Mormon emigrants on their way from the East to Caldwell County, turning them back in some instances, taking their arms from them in others, etc.

On the 29th, at Woolsey's, northeast of Breckenridge, an agreement was reached by the Gentiles for an attack upon Haun's mill. Their companies, numbering in the aggregate about two hundred men, were organized. They were commanded by Captains Nehemiah Comstock, William O. Jennings, and William Gee. The command of the battalion was given to Col. Thomas Jennings, an old militia officer, then living in the Forks. Nearly all the men were citizens of Livingston County. Perhaps twenty were from Daviess, from whence they had been driven by the Mormons during the troubles in that county a few weeks previously. The Daviess County men were very bitter against the Mormons, and vowed the direst vengeance on the entire sect. It did not matter whether or not the Mormons at the mill had taken any part in the disturbances which had occurred; it was enough that they were Mormons. The Livingston men became thoroughly imbued with the same spirit, and all were eager for the raid. The Livingston men had no wrongs to complain of themselves, for the Mormons had never invaded their county, or injured them in any way; but they seemed to feel an extraordinary sympathy for the outrages suffered by their neighbors.

Setting out from Woolsey's after noon on the 30th, Col. Jennings marched swiftly out of the timber northwest of the present village of Mooresville, and out on the prairie stretching down southwards toward the doomed hamlet at Haun's Mill. The word was passed along the column, "Shoot at everything wearing breeches, and shoot to kill."

All of the Gentiles were mounted, and they had with them a wagon and two Mormon prisoners. Within two miles of the mill the wagon and prisoners were left, in charge of a squad, and the remainder of the force pressed rapidly on. Entering the timber north of the mill, Colonel Jennings passed through it, unobserved, right up to the borders of the settlement, and speedily formed his line for the attack. Capt. W. O. Jennings' company had the center, Capt. Comstock's the left, and Capt. Gee's the right.

The Mormon leader had somehow become apprehensive of trouble. He communicated his fears to some of the men, and was about sending out scouts and pickets. It had been previously agreed that in case of attack the men should repair to the blacksmith shop and occupy it as a fort or blockhouse. This structure was built of logs, with wide cracks between them, was about eighteen feet square, and had a large wide door. The greater portion of the Mormons were, however, unsuspicious of any imminent peril. Children were playing

on the banks of the creek, women were engaged in their ordinary domestic duties, the newly arrived immigrants were resting under the trees, which were clad in the scarlet, crimson,
and golden leaves of autumn. The scene was peaceful and
Arcadian. It was now about four o'clock in the afternoon, and
the sun hung low and red in a beautiful Indian summer sky.

Suddenly, from out of the timber north and west of the
mill the Gentiles burst upon the hamlet. The air was filled
with shouts and shots, and the fight was on. It cannot fair-
ly be called a fight. Taken wholly by surprise, the Mormons
were thrown into extreme confusion. The women and children cried and screamed in excitement and terror, and the
greater number, directed by some of the men, ran across the
milldam to the south bank of the creek and sought shelter in
the woods. Perhaps twenty men, Captain Evans among
them, ran with their guns to the blacksmith shop and began
to return the fire. Some were shot down in their attempts to
reach the shop. The fire of the Mormons was wild and ineffective; that of the militia was accurate and deadly. The
cracks between the logs of the shop were so large that it was
easy to shoot through them, and so thickly were the Mormons huddled together on the inside that nearly every bullet which entered the shop killed or wounded a man. Firing
was kept up all the while on the fleeing fugitives, and many
were shot down as they ran.

Realizing very soon that he was placed at a decided disadvantage, Captain Evans gave orders to retreat, directing
every man to take care of himself. The door of the shop was
thrown open, and all of the able-bodied survivors ran out,
endeavoring to reach the woods. Some were shot before
reaching shelter. Captain Evans was much excited, and ran
all the way to Mud Creek, seven miles south, with his gun
loaded, not having discharged it during the fight. The Gentiles advanced, and began to use their rough, homemade

swords, or corn knives, with which some of them were armed. The fugitives were fired on until they were out of range, but not pursued, as the few who escaped scattered in almost every direction.

Coming upon the field after it had been abandoned, the Gentiles perpetrated some terrible deeds. At least three of the wounded were hacked to death with the "corn knives" or finished with a rifle bullet. William Reynolds, a Livingston County man, entered the blacksmith shop and found a little boy, only ten year of age, named Sardius Smith, hiding under the bellows. Without even demanding his surrender, the cruel wretch drew up his rifle and shot the little fellow as he lay cowering and trembling. Reynolds afterward boasted of his exploit to persons yet living. He described with fiendish glee how the poor child "kicked and squealed" in his dying agonies, and justified his inhuman act by the old Indian aphorism, "Nits will make lice." Charley Merrick, another little boy only nine years old, had hid under the bellows. He ran out, but did not get far until he received a load of buckshot and a rifle ball, in all three wounds. He did not die, however, for nearly five weeks. Esquire Thomas McBride was seventy-eight years of age, and had been a soldier under Gates and Washington in the Revolution.[4] He had started for the blacksmith shop, but was shot down on the way, and lay wounded and helpless, but still alive. A Daviess County man named Rogers, who kept a ferry across Grand River, near Gallatin, came upon him and demanded his gun. "Take it," said McBride. Rogers picked up the weapon and finding that it was loaded deliberately discharged it into the old veteran's breast. He then

---

[4] 4Though many accounts state that McBride was a veteran of the Revolutionary War, his son stated in his autobiography that he was born in 1776, making him 62 at the time of his death. McBride,James, "Autobiography of James McBride," typescript, Special Collections, Harold B Lee Library, BYU.

cut and hacked the body with his "corn knife" until it was frightfully gashed and mangled.

After the Mormons had all been either killed, wounded, or driven away, the Gentiles began to loot the place. Considerable property was taken, much of the spoil consisting of household articles and personal effects. At least three wagons and perhaps ten horses were taken. Two emigrant wagons were driven off with all their contents. The Mormons claim that there was a general pillage, and that even the bodies of the slain were robbed. The Gentiles deny this, and say that the wagons were needed to haul off their three wounded men, and the bedding was taken to make them comfortable, while the other articles taken did not amount to much. Two of the survivors have stated to me that the place was "pretty well cleaned out."

Colonel Jennings did not remain at the mill more than two hours. Twilight approaching, he set out on his return to his former encampment. He feared a rally and return of the Mormons with a large reinforcement, and doubtless he desired to reflect leisurely on his course of future operations. Reaching Woolsey's, he halted his battalion and prepared to pass the night. But a few hours later he imagined he heard cannon and a great tumult in the direction of Haun's Mill, betokening, as he thought, the advance of a large Mormon force upon him. Rousing his men from their sweet dream of the victory, he broke camp, moved rapidly eastward, and never halted until he had put the West Fork of Grand River between him and his imaginary pursuers. He and his men had won glory enough for one day, anyhow! They had not lost a man killed and only three wounded. John Renfrow had his thumb shot off, Allen England was shot in the thigh, and Hart in the arm.

The Mormons killed and mortally wounded numbered seventeen. Here are the names:

Thomas McBride, Augustine Harmer, Levi N. Merrick, Simon Cox, Elias Benner, Hiram Abbott, Josiah Fuller, John York, Benjamin Lewis, John Lee, Alexander Campbell, John Byers, George S. Richards, Warren Smith, William Napier, Charles Merrick, aged nine, Sardius Smith, aged 10.

The severely wounded numbered eleven men, one boy (Alma Smith, aged 7), and one woman, a Miss Mary Stedwell. The latter was shot through the hand and arm as she was running to the woods.

Dies iroe [*Dies irae*]—*on that day, dread day of wrath* Bloody work and woeful. What a scene did Colonel Jennings and his men turn their backs upon as they rode away in the gloaming from the little valley once all green and peaceful! The wounded men had been given no attention, and the bodies of the slain had been left to fester and putrefy in the Indian summer temperature, warm and mellowing. A large red moon rose, and a fog came up from the stream and lay like a face cloth upon the pallid countenances of the dead. Timidly and warily came forth the widows and orphans from their hiding places, and as they recognized one a husband, one after another a son, and another a brother among the slain, the wailings of grief and terror were most pitiful. All that night were they alone with their dead and wounded. There were no physicians, but if there had been many of the wounded, were past all surgery. Dreadful sights in the moonlight, and dreadful sounds on the night winds. In the hamlet the groans of the wounded, the moans and sobs of the grief-stricken, the bellowing of cattle, and the howling of dogs, and from the black woods the dismal hooting of owls.

By and by, when the wounded had been made as comfortable as possible, the few men who had returned gathered the women and children together, and all sought consolation. in prayer. Then they sang from the Mormon hymn book a selection entitled "Moroni's Lamentation," a dirge-like composition, lacking in poesy and deficient in rhythm, but giving something of comfort, let us hope, to the choristers. And so in prayer and song and ministration the remainder of the night was passed.

The next morning the corpses had changed, and were changing fast. There were not enough men left to make coffins or even dig graves. It could not be determined when relief would come or when the Gentiles would return. There was a large unfinished well near the mill, which it was decided should be used as a common sepulcher. Four men, one of whom was Joseph W. Young, a brother of Brigham Young, gathered up the bodies, the women assisting, and bore them, one at a time, on a large plank to the well, and slid them in. Some hay was strewn upon the ghastly pile and then a thin layer of dirt thrown upon the hay.

The next day Captain Comstock's company returned to the mill, as they said, to bury the dead. Finding that duty had been attended to, they expressed considerable satisfaction at having been relieved of the job, and after notifying the people that they must leave the State, or they would all be killed, they rode away. The pit was subsequently filled by Mr. C. R. Ross, now a resident of Black Oak, Caldwell County.

A day or two after the massacre, Colonel Jennings started with his battalion to join the State forces at Far West. He had not proceeded far when he met a messenger who informed him that the Mormons at Far West had surrendered, and gave him an order to move to Daviess county and join the forces under Gen. Robert Wilson then operating against the Mormons at Adam-ondi-ahman. The battalion was present at the surrender at "Diamo," as it is generally called, and a day or two thereafter Captain Comstock's company was ordered to Haun's mill, where it remained in camp for some weeks. Herewith I give an extract from an affidavit made by Mrs. Amanda Smith, whose husband and little son were killed in the massacre, and who resided in the mill during the stay of Comstock's company:—

". . . The next day the mob came back. They told us we must leave the State forthwith or be killed. It was bad weather, and they had taken our teams and clothes; our men were all dead or wounded. I told them they might kill me and my children, and welcome. They said to us, from time to time, if we did not leave the State they would come and kill us. We could not leave then. We had little prayer meetings; they said if we did not stop them they would kill every man, woman, and child. We had spelling schools for our little children; they pretended they were 'Mormon meetings,' and said if we did not stop them they would kill every man, woman, and child . . . I started the 1st of February, very cold weather, for Illinois, with five small children and no money. It was mob all the way. I drove the team, and we slept out of doors. We suffered greatly from hunger, cold, and fatigue; and for what? For our religion. In this boasted land of liberty, 'Deny your faith or die,' was the cry."

While in camp at the mill, according to the statements to me of two of its members, Comstock's company lived off the country, as did the State troops at Far West. The Mormon cattle and hogs had been turned into the fields and were fine and fat. The mill furnished flour and meal, and other articles of provision were to be had for the taking. The Mormon men were either prisoners, or had been driven from the country. By the 1st of April following all had left the State. Many of them had been killed, their houses burned, their property taken, their fields laid waste, and the result was called peace.

(Signed) Burr Joyce—pen name for Major Return S. Holcombe, written in 1887

There Were Not Enough Men
to Dig the Graves

Though the author of the following article is not given, it is found in the Reorganized Church of Jesus Christ of Latter-day Saints.[1] It is remarkably similar to the account in the previous chapter of this work. However, there are details in this chapter not found in the Holcombe account, which seems to be more polished and therefore may be an improvement on an earlier draft—perhaps this chapter.

❀   ❀   ❀

The foregoing statements are fully verified by the account given in the History of Caldwell and Livingston Counties, Missouri, with affidavits attached:—

In the afternoon of October 30, 1838, the day the militia arrived at Far West, occurred what has since been generally known as "the Haun's Mill Massacre." Following is perhaps the first complete and correct account of this affair ever published.

At Jacob Haun's mill, on the north bank of Shoal Creek, in the eastern part of the county in what is now Fairview Township (nw. 1/4 ne. 1/4 section 17-56-26), were besides the mill, a blacksmith shop and half a dozen or more houses, and perhaps twenty Mormon families. Some of these

---

[1] Smith III, *History of the Reorganized Church*, vol. 2, 237–44

families were living in tents and covered wagons, having recently come into the country, or having lived elsewhere in the county had become alarmed at the aspect of affairs, and had come to the mill for safety. News that the militia of the State had been ordered to expel them had reached the Mormons, and following these tidings word was brought that a considerable number of men living in Livingston County, together with some from Davies, had organized near Spring Hill, in Livingston County, and were preparing to attack them. A company of about thirty men, indifferently armed with shot guns and squirrel rifles, was organized, and David Evans, a Danite, was chosen captain. It was determined to defend the place.

Learning that the force organizing against them numbered some hundreds, some of the older men among the Mormons urged that no resistance should be made, but that all should retreat to Far West. It seems that the Prophet had advised this, but nevertheless had given them permission to remain if they thought they could protect themselves.

Others opposed retreating and the abandonment of their property to the "mob of Gentiles," and when an old man named Myers reminded them how few they were, and how many the Gentiles numbered, they declared that the Lord would send his angels to help them when the day of battle should come. Some of the women, too, urged the men to stand firm, and offered to mold bullets and prepare patching for the rifles if necessary.

North of Haun's mill, a short distance, was a body of timber and brush, and north of this, toward where Breckenridge now stands, was a stretch of prairie for miles. For a day or two Captain Evans kept a picket post in the northern edge of the timber, but having entered into a truce with Captain Nehemiah Comstock, commanding one of the Livingston

County companies, and no other enemy appearing, this post was withdrawn.

This truce was effected by means of a messenger, who rode between Comstock and Evans, and its terms were that the Gentiles were to let the Mormons alone as long as they were peaceable, and vice versa. The Mormons agreed also to disband their military organization if the Gentiles would disband theirs, and this it is claimed was agreed to. But the Mormons heard that over in Livingston, directly east of them, another company of Gentiles, under Captain William Mann, was menacing them; and so they did not disband; for while they confided in Comstock's company, they had no confidence in Mann's which for some time had been operating at and near Whitney's mill, on Shoal Creek (where Dawn now is), stopping Mormons on their way to Caldwell from the East, turning them back in some instances, taking their arms from them in others, etc. The Gentile force in Livingston County numbered about two hundred men, and was under the command of Colonel William O. Jennings, then the sheriff of that county. Three companies composed it, led by Captain Nehemiah Comstock, Thomas R. Bryan, and William Mann. It took the field in earnest about the 25th of October, and for a few days prior to the 30th was encamped about three miles northeast of Breckenridge, at least Comstock's company was. Perhaps Mann's was employed in the southern portion of the county until the 29th.

Learning that the Mormons at Haun's mill had not disbanded, and yielding to the almost universal desire of his men, who were eager to seize upon any pretext for a fight, Colonel Jennings set out from his camp last-mentioned, after noon of the 30th day of October, intending to attack and capture Haun's mill, and encamp there that night. The route lay via where Mooresville now stands, or between

Mooresville and Breckenridge, and on across the prairie, and the march was made swiftly and without interruption.

Within two miles of the mill Colonel Jennings left his wagons and two Mormon prisoners, captured some days before in charge of a squad of men, of whom James Trosper, now of Breckenridge, was one, and pressed rapidly on. Entering the timber north of the town, Jennings' men passed through it unobserved right up to the borders of the hamlet. Captain Nehemiah Comstock's company had the advance.

The Mormon leader, David Evans, had become apprehensive of an attack, and was about sending out scouts and pickets. It was arranged to use the blacksmith shop as a fort or blockhouse. This structure was of logs, with wide cracks between them, and had a large door. The greater portion of the Mormons were unsuspicious of imminent danger, and the women and children were scattered about. Nearly every house contained two or more families. There were two or three small houses on the south bank of the creek thus occupied. It was now about four o'clock in the afternoon of a warm and beautiful Indian summer day.

Suddenly from out of the timber north of the mill the Livingston militia burst upon the hamlet. In a few seconds the air was filled with wild shouts and shots, and the fight was on. It can scarcely be called a fight. The Mormons were thrown into confusion and many of them ran wildly and aimlessly about. The women and children cried and screamed in excitement and terror, and the greater number, directed by the men, ran across the milldam to the south bank and sought shelter in the woods south of the creek. Perhaps half of the men, Evans among them, ran with their guns to the blacksmith shop and began to return the fire. Some were shot down in an effort to reach the shop or as they were trying to escape.

The fire of the Mormons was for the most part wild and ineffective; that of the militia was accurate and deadly. The cracks between the logs of the shop were so large that it was easy to shoot through them, and so thickly were the Mormons huddled together on the inside that nearly every bullet that entered the shop killed or wounded a man. Firing was kept up all the while on the fleeing fugitives, many of whom were shot down.

Seeing that he was placed at a decided disadvantage, Captain Evans gave orders to retreat, ordering every man to take care of himself. The door of the shop was thrown open and all the able-bodied survivors ran out, endeavoring to reach the wood. Some were shot before they got to shelter. Captain Evans was somewhat excited, and, as he afterwards related, ran all the way to Mud Creek with his gun loaded, not having fired it during the fight. The militia fired at the fugitives until they were out of range, but did not pursue them, as the few who escaped scattered in almost every direction.

After the engagement was over and all the able-bodied male Mormons had been killed, wounded, or driven away, some of the militiamen began to "loot" the houses and stables at the mill. A great deal of property was taken, much of it consisting of household articles and personal effects, but just how much cannot now be stated. The Mormons claim there was a general pillage and that in two or three instances the bodies of the slain were robbed. Some of the militia or their friends say only two or three wagons were taken, one to haul off the three wounded, and sufficient bedding to make their ride comfortable; but on the other hand two of those who were in a position to know say that the Mormon hamlet was pretty thoroughly rifled. One man carried away an empty ten gallon keg, which he carried before him on his saddle and beat as a drum. Another had a woman's bonnet, which he said was for his sweetheart. Perhaps a dozen horses were taken.

Colonel Jennings did not remain at Haun's mill, in all, more than an hour or an hour and a half. Twilight approaching, he set out on his return to his former camp, for one reason fearing a rally and return of the Mormons with a large reinforcement, and doubtless desiring to reflect leisurely on his course of future operations.

Reaching his camp near Woolsey's, northeast of Breckenridge, Colonel Jennings halted his battalion and prepared to pass the night. But a few hours later he imagined he heard cannon and a great tumult in the direction of Haun's mill, betokening the presence of a large Mormon force, and rousing up his men he broke camp, and moving rapidly eastward never halted until he had put the west fork of Grand River between him and his imaginary pursuers!

From the records of the Mormon Church it seems that seventeen men of the Mormons were either killed outright or mortally wounded. Their names, as kindly furnished for this history by Rev. F. D. Richards, assistant historian and custodian of the church records at Salt Lake, are:—

Thos. McBride, Alex. Campbell, Hiram Abbott
Levi N. Merrick, Geo. S. Richards, John York
Elias Benner, Wm. Napier, John Lee
Josiah Fuller, Augustine Harmer, John Byers
Benj. Lewis, Simon Cox, Warren Smith
Sardius Smith, aged 10, and Chas. Merrick, aged 9.

Esq. Thomas McBride was an old soldier of the Revolution. He was lying wounded and helpless, his gun by his side. A militiaman named Rogers came up to him and demanded it. 'Take it,' said McBride. Rogers picked up the weapon, and finding that it was loaded, deliberately discharged it into the old man's breast. He then cut and hacked the old veteran's body with a rude sword, or "corn knife," until it was frightfully mangled. William Reynolds, a Livingston County man, killed the little boy Sardius Smith, ten years of age. The lad had run into the blacksmith shop and crawled under the bellows for safety. Upon entering the shop the cruel militiaman discovered the cowering, trembling little fellow, and without even demanding his surrender fired upon and killed him, and afterwards boasted of the atrocious deed to Charles R. Ross and others. He described, with fiendish glee, how the boy struggled in his dying agony, and justified his savage and inhuman conduct in killing a mere child by saying, "Nits will make lice, and if he had lived he would have become a Mormon."

Charlie Merrick, another little Mormon boy, was mortally wounded by another militiaman. He too was hiding under the bellows.

The Mormons wounded, according to the Mormon records, numbered twelve, as follows:—Isaac Laney, Wm. Yokum, Jacob Potts, Nathan K. Knight, Tarlton Lewis, Chas. Jimison, Jacob Myers, Jacob Haun, John Walker, George Myers, Jacob Foutz, Alma Smith, aged 7.

A young Mormon woman, Miss Mary Stedwell, was shot through the hand, as she was running to the woods. Doubtless this shooting was accidental.

The militia or Jennings' men, had but three men wounded, and none killed. John Renfrow, now living in Ray County, had a thumb shot off. Allen England, a Daviess County man, was severely wounded in the thigh, and the other wounded man was named Hart.

Dies iroe! [*sic*] [*On that day, dread day of wrath,*] What a woeful day this had been to Haun's Mill. What a pitiful scene was there when the militia rode away upon the conclusion of their bloody work! The wounded men had been given no attention, and the bodies of the slain were left to fester and putrefy in the Indian summer temperature, warm and mellowing. The widows and orphans of the dead came timidly and warily forth from their hiding places as soon as the troops left, and as they recognized one a husband, another a father, another a son, another a brother among the bloody corpses, the wailings of grief and terror that went up were pitiful and agonizing. All that night they were alone with their dead. A return visit of Jennings' men to complete the work of "extermination" had been threatened and was expected. Verily the experience of the poor survivors of the Haun's Mill affair was terrible, no wonder that they long remembered it.

The next morning the bodies had changed, and were changing fast. They must be buried. There were not enough men in the place to dig graves, and it could not be determined when relief would come. There was a large unfinished well at the place, and the bodies were gathered up, the women assisting, and borne, one at a time, all gory and ghastly, to this well and slid in from a large plank. All of the corpses were disposed of in this way; then some hay or straw was strewn over the ghastly piles and then a thin layer of dirt thrown on the hay.

Soon after the burial was over, the same day, Comstock's company was sent back to give the dead a decent sepulture. Seeing what had been done already, they rode away, glad to be relieved from the job. The next February Mr. Charles R. Ross moved into the house and occupied the property to which the well belonged. Soon after his arrival some warm days came, and an offensive smell arose from the well. Mr. Ross at once set to work and filled up the loathsome sepulcher, even making a good sized mound over it. In time this mount was leveled, and now it is almost impossible to fix the exact location of the pit.

Whatever of merit there was in the attack on Haun's Mill, and whatever of glory attaches to the famous victory, must be given to Colonel William O. Jennings mainly. He made the attack on his own responsibility, without orders from Governor Boggs, or any other superior authority, although the Governor afterwards approved what was done. True, Jennings' subordinates must be given their share, in proportion to the part they bore, but Colonel Jennings stands among them all as a Saul among his fellows, the Ajax Telamon of the contest, the hector of the fight!

It is but proper that both sides of the story of the affair at Haun's Mill fight, skirmish, massacre, or butchery, whatever it was—should be given. The best Mormon account extant is embodied in an affidavit of Joseph Young, a brother of Brigham Young, made at Quincy, Illinois, the June following the occurrence. This affidavit, much of which is undoubtedly true, is yet among the Mormon records, and a copy has been furnished for use in this history by F.D. Richards, the Mormon custodian of records. Following is the copy. [*Joseph Young's journal follows in the next chapter. Ed.*]

3

Joseph Young's Narration

*I was not willing . . . to abandon my object which
was to locate myself and family in a fine, healthy country.*

Joseph Young, son of John and Nabbie (Howe) Young, was born
on April 7, 1797, in Hopkinton, Middlesex County, Massachusetts. He was converted to the Mormon faith by his brother,
Brigham Young, and was baptized on April 6, 1832. He married
June Adeline Bickness on February 18, 1834, and she bore him eleven
children. He was driven out of Missouri to Illinois, where he united with his brother, Brigham, thereafter going to Salt Lake City,
where he died on July 16, 1881.[1] The statement has been published
many times.[2]

❀   ❀   ❀

On the sixth day of July last, I started with my family from
Kirtland, Ohio, for the state of Missouri, the county of
Caldwell, in the upper part of the state, being the place of
my destination.

On the thirteenth day of October I crossed the Mississippi at Louisiana, at which place I heard vague reports of
the disturbances in the upper country, but nothing that
could be relied upon. I continued my course westward till I
crossed Grand river, at a place called Compton's ferry, at
which place I heard, for the first time, that if I proceeded

---

[1]Smith Jr., *History of the Church*, vol. 7, 187.
[2]The transcription in this work is from Smith Jr., *History of the Church*, vol. 3,
1883–1886.

any farther on my journey, I would be in danger of being stopped by a body of armed men. I was not willing, however, while treading my native soil, and breathing republican air, to abandon my object, which was to locate myself and family in a fine, healthy country, where we could enjoy the society of our friends and connections. Consequently, I prosecuted my journey till I came to Whitney's Mills, situated on Shoal creek, in the eastern part of Caldwell county.

After crossing the creek and going about three miles, we met a party of the mob, about forty in number, armed with rifles, and mounted on horses, who informed us that we could go no farther west, threatening us with instant death if we proceeded any farther. I asked them the reason of this prohibition; to which they replied, that we were "Mormons:" that everyone who adhered to our religious faith, would have to leave the state in ten days, or renounce their religion. Accordingly they drove us back to the mills above mentioned.

Here we tarried three days; and, on Friday, the twenty-sixth, we recrossed the creek, and following up its banks, we succeeded in eluding the mob for the time being, and gained the residence of a friend in Myer's settlement.

On Sunday, twenty-eighth October, we arrived about twelve o'clock, at Haun's Mills, where we found a number of our friends collected together, who were holding a council, and deliberating on the best course for them to pursue, to defend themselves against the mob, who were collecting in the neighborhood under the command of Colonel Jennings, of Livingston county, and threatening them with house burning and killing. The decision for the council was, that our friends there should place themselves in an attitude of self defense. Accordingly about twenty-eight of our men armed themselves, and were in constant readiness for an attack of any small body of men that might come down upon them.

The same evening, for some reason best known to themselves, the mob sent one of their number to enter into a treaty with our friends, which was accepted, on the condition of mutual forbearance on both sides, and that each party, as far as their influence extended, should exert themselves to prevent any further hostilities upon either party.

At this time, however, there was another mob collecting on Grand River, at William Mann's who were threatening us, consequently we remained under arms.

Monday passed away without molestation from any quarter.

On Tuesday, the 30th, that blood tragedy was acted, the name of which I shall never forget. More than three-fourths of the day had passed in tranquility, as smiling as the preceding one. I think there was no individual of our company that was apprised of the sudden and awful fate that hung over our heads like an overwhelming torrent, which was to change the prospects, the feelings and the circumstances of about thirty families. The banks of Shoal creek on either side teemed with children sporting and playing, while their mothers were engaged in domestic employments, and their fathers employed in guarding the mills and other property, while others were engaged in gathering in their crops for their winter consumption. The wether was very pleasant, the sun shone clear, all was tranquil, and no one expressed any apprehension of the awful crisis that was near us—even at our doors.

It was about four o'clock, while sitting in my cabin with my babe in my arms, and my wife standing by my side, the door being open. I cast my eyes on the opposite bank of Shoal creek and saw a large company of armed men, on horses, directing their course towards the mills with all possible speed. As they advanced through the scattering trees that stood on the edge of the prairie they seemed to form themselves into a three square position, forming a vanguard in front.

At this moment, David Evans, seeing the superiority of their numbers, (there being two hundred and forty of them, according to their own account), swung his hat, and cried for peace. This not being heeded, they continued to advance, and their leader, Mr. Nehemiah Comstock, fired a gun, which was followed by a solemn pause of ten or twelve seconds, when, all at once, they discharged about one hundred rifles, aiming at a blacksmith shop into which our friends had fled for safety and charged up to the shop, the cracks of which between the logs were sufficiently large to enble them to aim directly at the bodies of those who had there fled for refuge from the fire of their murderers. There were several families tented in the rear of the shop, whose lives were exposed, and amidst a shower of bullets fled to the woods in different directions.

After standing and gazing on this bloody scene for a few minutes, and finding myself in the uttermost danger, the bullets having reached the house where I was living, I committed my family to the protection of heaven, and leaving the house on the opposite side, I took a path which led up the hill, following in the trail of three of my brethren that had fled from the shop. While ascending the hill we were discovered by the mob, who immediately fired at us, and continued so to do till we reached the summit. In descending the hill, I secreted myself in a thicket of bushes, where I lay till eight o'clock in the evening, at which time I heard a female voice calling my name in an under tone, telling me that the mob had gone and there was no danger. I immediately left the thicket, and went to the house of Benjamin Lewis, where I found my family (who had fled there) in safety, and two of my friends mortally wounded, one of whom died before morning. Here we passed the painful night in deep and awful reflections on the scenes of the preceding evening.

After daylight appeared, some four or five men, who with myself, had escaped with our lives from the horrid massacre, and who repaired as soon as possible to the mills, to learn the condition of our friends, whose fate we had but too truly anticipated. When we arrived at the house of Mr. Haun, we found Mr. Merrick's body lying in the rear of the house, Mr. McBride's in front, literally mangled from head to feet. We were informed by Miss Rebecca Judd, who was an eye witness, that he was shot with his own gun, after he had given it up, and then cut to pieces with a corn cutter by a Mr. Rogers of Daviess county, who keeps a ferry on Grand River, and who has since repeatedly boasted of this act of savage barbarity. Mr. York's body we found in the house, and after viewing these corpses, we immediately went to the blacksmith's shop, where we found nine of our friends, eight of whom were already dead; the other, Mr. Cox, of Indiana, struggling in the agonies of death and soon expired. We immediately prepared and carried them to the place of internment. The last office of kindness due to the remains of departed friends, was not attended with the customary ceremonies or decency, for we were in jeopardy, every moment expecting to be fired upon by the mob, who, we supposed, were lying in ambush, waiting for the first opportunity to despatch the remaining few who were providentially preserved from the slaughter of the preceding day. However, we accomplished without molestation this painful task. The place of burying was a vault in the ground, formerly intended for a well, into which we threw the bodies of our friends promiscuously. Among those slain I will mention Sardius Smith, son of Warren Smith, about nine years old, who through fear, had crawled under the bellows in the shop, where he remained til the massacre was over, when he was discovered by a Mr. Glaze, of Carroll county, who presented his rifle near the boy's head, and literally blowed off the upper part of it. Mr. Stanley of Carroll, told me afterwards that Glaze boasted of this fiend-like murder and heroic deed all over the country.

The number killed and mortally wounded in this wanton slaughter was eighteen or nineteen, whose names as far as I recollect were as follows: Thomas McBride, Levi N. Merrick, Elias Benner, Josiah Fuller, Benjamin Lewis, Alexander Campbell, Warren Smith, Sardius Smith, George S. Richards, Mr. William Napier, Augustine Harmer, Simon Cox, Mr. (Hiram) Abbott, John York, Charles Merrick, (a boy eight or nine years old), (John Lee, John Byers), and three or four others whose names I do not recollect, as they were strangers, to me. Among the wounded who recovered were Issac Laney, Nathan K. Knight, Mr. (William) Yokum, two brothers by the name of (Jacob and George) Myers, Tarlton Lewis, Mr. (Jacob) Haun, and several others, (Jacob Foutz, Jacob Potts, Charles Jimison, John Walker, Alma Smith, aged about nine years). Miss Mary Stedwell, while fleeing, was shot through the hand, and, fainting, fell over a log, into which they shot upwards of twenty balls.

To finish their work of destruction, this band of murderers, composed of men from Daviess, Livingston, Ray, Carroll, and Chariton counties, led by some of the principal men of that section of the of the upper country, (according whom I am informed were Mr. Ashby, or Chariton, member of the state legislature; Colonel Jennings, of Livingston county, Thomas O. Bryon, clerk of Livingston county; Mr. Whitney, Dr. Randall, and many others), proceeded to rob the houses, wagons, and tents, of bedding and clothing; drove off horses and wagons, leaving widows and orphans destitute of the necessities of life; and even stripped the clothing from the bodies of the slain. According to their own account, they fired seven rounds in this awful butchery, making upwards of sixteen hundred shots at a little company of men, about thirty in number. I hereby certify the above to be a true statement of facts, according to the best of my knowledge.

Joseph Young

State of Illinois)   ss.
County of Adams)

    I hereby certify that Joseph Young this day came before me, and made oath in due form of law, that the statements contained in the foregoing sheet are true, according to the best of his knowledge and belief. In testimony whereof I have hereunto set my hand and affixed the seal of the Circuit Court at Quincy, this fourth day of June, in the year of our Lord one thousand eight hundred and thirty-nine.

C. M. Woods,
Clerk Circuit Court, Adams Co. Ill.

4

Amanda Smith:
"Deny Your Faith or Die"

*A*manda Barnes Smith (*1809–1886*) was born at Becket, Berkshire County, Massachusetts. She married Warren Smith in Lorain County, Ohio, in *1826* and converted to Mormonism in *1831*. Following her experiences in Missouri, she relocated to Nauvoo, Illinois, and migrated to Utah in *1850*. She resided in Salt Lake City until shortly before her death, when she went to live with a daughter at Richmond, Cache County, Utah. Her agony and sorrow resulting from the tragedy at Haun's Mill are almost impossible to comprehend. After losing her husband and one son, she sought to care for another son whose hip was badly wounded. No doctors were available, nor were medical supplies, yet Amanda's faith enabled her to heal her son's leg. Her tremendous courage impressed the mobbers, who eventually allowed her to leave the state of Missouri. Following are two accounts in her own words of that dreadful day. The first was written as an affidavit and registered with the clerk of Adams County to be submitted as part of the Mormons' appeal to the government for legal redress. The second account gives more detail and was written at a later date for her family and friends.[1]

❧　　❧　　❧

---

[1]Both accounts are found in Paul W. Hodson, *Never Forsake: The Story of Amanda Barnes Smith—Legacy of the Haun's Mill Massacre* (Salt Lake City: Keeban Productions, 1996), 67–87 and 238–41. The first account can also be found in Smith Jr., *History of the Church*, vol. 3, 323–25; the second account, with some repetition but more detail, is given in Tullidge, *Women of Mormondom*, 121–32.

To Whom This May Come,

I do hereby certify, that my husband, Warren Smith, in company with several other families, while moving from Ohio to Missouri, late last fall (1838), we came to Caldwell County. Whilst we were traveling, and minding our own businesses we were stopped by a mob; they told us that if we went another step they would kill us all. Then they took our guns from us. (As we were going into a new country we took guns along with us.) They took us back five miles, placed a guard around us, and there kept us three days, then let us go.

I thought to myself is this our boasted land of liberty? For some said that we must deny our faith or they would kill us, others said we should die at any rate.

The names of the heads of this mob were Thomas O'Brian, County Clerk, Jefferson Brion, William Ewell, Esq., James Austin, all of Livingston County, Mo. After they let us go, we traveled ten miles when we came to a small town, composed of one grist mill and one saw mill, and eight or ten houses belonging to our brethren. Here we stopped for the night. A little before sunset (October 30, 1838) a mob of three hundred persons came upon us. The men hollered for the women and children to run for the woods, and they ran into an old blacksmith shop, where they feared, that if we all ran together, they would rush upon us, and kill the women and children. The mob fired before we had time to run from our camp. Our men then took off their hats and swung them around and cried, "quarter, quarter" until they were shot down. The mob paid no attention to their cries nor entreaties but fired incessantly.

I took my little girls (my boys I could not find) and started for the woods. The mob encircled us on all sides except towards the brook. I ran down the bank, across the mill pond on a plank, up the hill into the bushes. The bullets whistled around us all the way like hail, and cut down the bushes on all sides of us. One girl (Mary Stedwell) was wounded by my side and fell over a log; her clothes hung across the log, and they shot at them expecting that they were hitting her, and our people afterwards cut out of that log twenty bullets.

I sat down and witnessed the dreadful scene. When they had done firing, they began to howl and one would have thought that all the infernals had come from the lower regions. They plundered the principal parts of our goods, took our horses and wagons and then ran off howling like demons.

I then came down to view the awful sight. Oh Horrible! What a sight! My husband, and one son (Sardius), ten years old, lay lifeless on the ground, and another son (Alma) badly wounded seven years old; the grounds covered with the dead. These little boys had crept under the bellows in the shop. Another boy (Charles Merrick) ten years old had three wounds in him, he lived five weeks and then died. He was not mine.

Realize for a moment the scene. It was sunset, nothing but horror and distress. The dogs filled with rage, howling over their dead masters, whilst the cattle caught the scent of the innocent blood and bellowed most awfully. A dozen helpless widows, thirty or forty fatherless children crying and groaning the loss of their husbands and fathers, the groans of the wounded and dying, was enough to melt the heart of anything but a Missouri mob.

Fifteen were dead, and ten wounded or more, two of whom died the next day. The women were not able to bury the dead, so they were thrown into a dry well and covered with dirt. The next day the mob came back. They told us, that we must leave the state forthwith or be killed. It was cold weather, and they had our teams and clothes, our men all dead or wounded. I told them that they might kill me and my children and welcome, they sent to us from time to time, that if we did not leave the state they would come and kill us. We had little prayer meetings. They said, if we did not stop them they would kill everyone of us, man, woman, and child, we had spelling schools for our little children, and they said we must also stop them. We did our own milking, and got our own wood, no man to help us.

I started on the first of February (1839) for Illinois, without money, (mob all the way) drove my own team, slept out of doors; I had four small children. We suffered hunger, fatigue and cold. And for what? For our religion, where? In a boasted land of liberty. "Deny your faith or die," was the cry.

I will mention some of the names of the heads of the mob. Two brothers by the name of Comstock, William Mann, Benjamin Ashley, Robert White, and one by the name of Rogers who took an old scythe and cut an old white headed man (Thomas McBride) all to pieces.

I wish also further to state when the mob came back there (and was told by one of them afterwards) their intention was to kill everything belonging to us that had life; and that after our men were shot down by them, they went all around and shot all the dead men over again to make sure of their death.

I will leave it with this Honorable Government to say what my damage may be; or what they would be willing to see their wives and children slaughtered for, as I have seen my husband, son and others.

I lost in property by the mob—to goods stolen, fifty dollars; one pocket book and fifty dollar cash notes; damages of horse and time, one hundred dollars, one gun and ten dollars, in short my all. Whole damages are more than the State of Missouri is worth.

Written by my own hand in truth on this eighteenth day of April 1839.

Amanda Smith

The preceding affidavit was registered with the clerk of Adams County and submitted as part of the Mormons' appeal to the government for legal redress.

The account was written a year after the massacre in an attempt to get necessary monetary aid. Notice how she doesn't mention the death of her husband and one son, and the suffering of another son, when she asks for restitution. A monetary value could never compensate for her loss.

❀   ❀   ❀

Amanda Smith wrote the following account forty years later for her children and her people.

We sold our beautiful home in Kirtland for a song, and traveled all summer to Missouri—our teams poor, and with hardly enough to keep body and soul together.

We arrived in Caldwell County, near Haun's Mill, nine wagons of us in company (as a subgroup of Kirtland Camp). Two days before we arrived we were taken prisoners by an armed mob that had demanded every bit of ammunition and every weapon we had. We surrendered all. They knew it, for they searched our wagons.

A few miles more brought us to Haun's Mill, where that awful scene of murder was enacted. My husband pitched his tent by a blacksmith's shop.

Brother David Evans made a treaty with the mob that they would not molest us. He came just before the massacre and called the company together and they knelt in prayer.

I sat in my tent. Looking up I suddenly saw the mob coming—the same that took away our weapons. They came like to many demons or wild Indians.

Before I could get to the blacksmith's shop door to alarm the brethren, who were at prayers, the bullets were whistling amongst them.

I seized my two little girls and escaped across the millpond on a slab-walk. Mary Stedwell fled with me. Yet though we were women, with tender children, in flight for our lives, the demons poured volley after volley to kill us.

A number of bullets entered my clothes, but I was not wounded. Mary cried out that she was hit. We had just reached the trunk of a fallen tree, over which I urged her, bidding her to shelter there where the bullets could not reach her, while I continued my flight to some bottom land.

When the firing had ceased I went back to the scene of the massacre, for there were my husband and three sons, of whose fate I as yet knew nothing.

As I returned I found Mary in a pool of blood where she had fainted, but she was only shot through the hand. Farther on was lying dead Brother McBride, an aged white-haired revolutionary soldier. His murderer had literally cut him to pieces with an old corn-cutter. His hands had been split down when he raised them in supplication for mercy. Then the monster cleft open his head with the same weapon, and the veteran who had fought for his country, in the glorious days of the past, was numbered with the martyrs.

Passing on I came to a scene more terrible still to the mother and wife. Emerging from the blacksmith shop was Willard, bearing on his shoulders his little brother Alma.

"Oh! My Alma is dead!" I cried, in anguish.

"No, mother; I think Alma is not dead. But father and brother Sardius are killed!"

What an answer was this to appall me! My husband and son murdered; another little son seemingly mortally wounded; and perhaps before the dreadful night should pass the murdered would return and complete their work!

But I could not weep then. The fountain of tears was dry; the heart overburdened with its calamity, and all the mother's sense absorbed in its anxiety for the precious boy which God alone could save by his miraculous aid.

The entire hip joint of my wounded boy had been shot away. Flesh, hip bone, joint and all had been ploughed from the muzzle of the gun which the ruffian placed to the child's hip through the logs of the hop and deliberately fired. The bones that remained were three or four inches apart.

We laid little Alma on a bed in our tent and I examined the wound. It was a ghastly sight. I knew not what to do. It was night now.

There were none left from that terrible scene, throughout that long, dark night, but about half a dozen bereaved and lamenting women, and the children. Eighteen or nineteen, all grown men excepting my murdered boy and another about the same age, were dead or dying; several more of the men were wounded, hiding away, those groans through the night too well disclosed their hiding places, while the rest of the men had fled, at the moment of the massacre, to save their lives.

The women were sobbing, in the greatest anguish of spirit; the children were crying loudly with fear and grief at the loss of fathers, and brothers, the dogs howled over their dead masters and the cattle were terrified with the scene of the blood of the murdered.

Yet was I there, all that long, dreadful night, with my dead and my wounded, and none but God as our physician and help.

Oh, my Heavenly Father, I cried. What shall I do? Thou seest my poor wounded boy and knowest my inexperience. Oh Heavenly Father, direct me what to do!

And then I was directed as by a voice speaking to me.

The ashes of our fire was still smoldering. We had been burning the bark of the shag-bark hickory. I was directed to take those ashes and make a lye and put a cloth saturated with it right into the wound. It hurt, but little Alma was too near dead to heed it much. Again and again I saturated the cloth and put it into the hole from which the hip joint had been ploughed, and each time mashed flesh and splinters of bone came away with the cloth; and the wound became as white as chicken's flesh.

Having done as directed I again prayed to the Lord and was again instructed as distinctly as though a physician had been standing by speaking to me.

Nearby was a slippery-elm tree. From this I was told to make a slippery-elm poultice and fill the wound with it. Willard got the slippery-elm roots, I made the poultice, and the wound, which took fully a quarter of a yard of linen to cover, so large was it, was properly dressed.

It was then I found vent to my feelings in tears, and resigned myself to the anguish of the hour. And all that night we, a few poor, stricken women, were thus left there with our dead and wounded. All through the night we heard the groans of the dying. Once in the dark we crawled over the heap of dead in the blacksmith's shop to try to help or soothe the sufferers' wants; once we followed the cries of a wounded brother who hid in some bushes from the murderers, and relieved him all we could.

It has passed from my memory whether he was dead in the morning or whether he recovered.

Next morning brother Joseph Young came to the scene of the massacre.

"What shall be done with the dead?" he inquired, in horror and deep trouble.

There was not time to bury them for the mob was coming on us. Neither were there left men to dig the graves. All the men excepting the two or three who had so narrowly escaped were dead or wounded. It had been no battle, but a massacre indeed.

"Do anything, Brother Joseph," I said, "rather than leave their bodies to the fiends who have killed them."

There was a deep dry well close by. Into this the bodies had to be hurried, eighteen or nineteen in number.

No funeral service could be performed, nor could they be buried with customary decency. The lives of those who in terror performed the last duty to the dead were in jeopardy. Every moment we expected to be fired upon by the fiends who we supposed were lying in ambush waiting the first opportunity to dispatch the remaining few who had escaped the slaughter of the preceding day. So in the hurry and terror of the moment some were thrown into the well head downwards and some feet downwards.

But when it came to the burial of my murdered boy, Sardius, Brother Joseph Young, who was assisting to carry him on a board to the well, laid down the corpse and declared that he could not throw the boy into this horrible grave. All the way on that journey, that summer, Joseph had played with my lad who had been so cruelly murdered. It was too much for one whose nature was so tender as Uncle Joseph's, and whose sympathies by this time were quite over-wrought. He could not perform that last office. My murdered son was left unburied.

"Oh! They have left my Sardius unburied in the sun," I cried, and ran and got a sheet and covered his body.

There he lay until the next day, and then I, his mother, assisted by his elder brother, had to throw him into the well. Straw and earth were thrown into this rude vault to cover the dead.

Sardius and Alma had crawled under the bellows in the blacksmith's shop. Willard had run to the blacksmith shop, with them, but instead of going in, had run around the back where he hid in a pile of wood, thereby saving his life. Alma's hip was shot away while thus hiding. Sardius was discovered after the massacre by the monsters who came in to despoil the bodies. In cold blood, one Glaze, of Carroll

County, presented a rifle near the head of Sardius and literally blew off the upper part of it, leaving the skull empty and dry while the brains and hair of the murdered boy were scattered around and on the walls.

At this one of the men, more merciful than the rest, observed: "It was a damned shame to kill those little boys."

"Damn the difference!" retorted the other. "Nits make lice!"

Willard saw the mobocrat William Mann take from my husband's feet before he was dead, a pair of new boots. The ruffian dragged his father across the shop in the act of pulling off his boot.

"Oh, you have hurt me!" groaned my husband, but the murderer dragged him back again, pulling off the other boot; "and there," says the boy, "my father fell over dead."

Afterwards this William Mann showed the boots on his own feet in Far West, saying: "Here is a pair of boots that I pulled off before the damned Mormon was done kicking!"

The murderer Glaze also boasted over the country, as a heroic deed, the blowing off the head of my young son.

But to return to Alma, and how the Lord helped me to safe his life.

I removed the wounded boy to the house of Brother David Evans, two miles away, the next day, and dressed his hip; the Lord directing me as before. I was reminded that in my husband's trunk there was a bottle of balsam. This I poured into the wound, greatly soothing Alma's pain.

"Alma, my child," I said, "you believe that the Lord made your hip?"

"Yes, Mother."

"Well, the Lord can make something there in the place of your hip. Don't you believe that he can, Alma?"

"Do you think that the Lord can, Mother?" inquired the child, in his simplicity.

"Yes, my son," I replied, "he has shown it all to me in a vision."

Then I laid him comfortably on his face and said, "Now you lay like that, and don't move, and the Lord will make you another hip."

So Alma laid on his face for five weeks, until he was entirely recovered—a flexible gristle having grown in place of the missing joint and socket, which remains to this day a marvel to physicians.

On the day that he walked again I was out of the house fetching a bucket of water, when I heard screams from the children. Running back, in affright, I entered, and there was Alma on the floor, dancing around, and the children screaming in astonishment and joy.

It is now nearly forty years ago, but Alma has never been the least crippled during his life, and he has traveled quite a long period of the time as a missionary of the gospel and a living miracle of the power of God.

I cannot leave the tragic story without relating some incidents of those five weeks when I was a prisoner with my wounded boy in Missouri, near the scene of the massacre, unable to obey the order of extermination.

All the Mormons in the neighborhood had fled out of the state, excepting a few families of the bereaved women and children who had gathered at the house of Brother David Evans. To this house Alma had been carried after that fatal night.

In our utter desolation what could we women do but pray? Prayer was our only source of comfort, our Heavenly Father our only helper. None but he could save and deliver us.

One day a mobber came from the mill with the Captain's fiat: "The captain says if you women don't stop your damned praying he will send down a posse and kill every damned one of you!"

And he might as well have done it, as to stop us poor women praying in that hour of our great calamity. Our prayers were hushed in terror. We dared not let our voices be heard in the house in supplication I could pray in my bed or in silence, but I could not live thus long. This godless silence was more intolerable than had been that night of the massacre.

I could bear it no longer. I pined to hear once more my own voice in petition to my Heavenly Father. I stole down into a corn-field and crawled into a stock of corn. It was as the temple of the Lord to me at that moment. I prayed aloud and most fervently.

When I emerged from the corn a voice spoke to me. It was a voice as plain as I ever heard one. It was no silent, strong impression of the spirit, but a voice, repeating a verse of our hymn:

> The soul who on Jesus hath leaned for repose,
>   I cannot, I will not desert to his foes;
> That soul, though all hell should endeavor to shake,
>   I'll never, no never, no never forsake!

From that moment I had no more fear. I felt that nothing could hurt me. Soon after this, the mob sent us word that unless we were all out of the State by a certain day we should be killed.

The day came, and at evening came fifty armed men to execute the sentence.

I met them at the door. They demanded of me why I was not gone? I bade them enter and see their own work. They crowded into my room and I showed them my wounded boy. They came, party after party, until all had seen my excuse. Then they quarreled among themselves and came near fighting.

At last they went away, all but two. These I thought were detailed to kill us. Then the two returned.

"Madam," said one, "have you any meat in the house?"

"No," was my reply.

"Could you dress a fat hog if one was laid at your door?"

"I think we could!" was my answer.

And then they went and caught a fat hog from a herd which had belonged to a now exiled brother, killed it and dragged it to my door, and departed.

These men, who had come to murder us, left on the threshold of our door a met offering to atone for their repented intention.

Yet even when my son was well I could not leave the State, now accursed indeed to the saints.

The mob had taken my horses, as they had the drove of horses, and the beeves, and the hogs, and wagons, and the tents, of the murdered and exiled.

So I went down into Davies county (ten miles) to Captain Comstock, and demanded of him my horses. There was one of them in his yard. He said I could have it if I paid five dollars for its keep. I told him I had no money.

I did not fear the captain of the mob, for I had the Lord's promise that nothing should hurt me. But his wife swore that the mobbers were fools for not killing the women and children as well as the men—declaring that we would "breed up a pack ten times worse than the first."

I left without the captain's permission to take my horse, or giving pay for its keep; but I went into his yard and took it, and returned to our refuge unmolested.

Learning that my other horse was at the mill, I next yoked up a pair of steers to a sled and went and demanded it also.

Comstock was there at the mill. He gave me the horse, and then asked if I had any flour.

"No, we have had none for weeks."

He then gave me about fifty pounds of flour and some beef, and filled a can with honey.

But the mill, and the slaughtered beeves which hung plentifully on its walls, and the stock of flour and honey, and abundant spoil besides, had all belonged to the murdered or exiled saints.

Yet was I thus providentially, by the very murderers and mobocrats themselves, helped out of the state of Missouri.

The Lord had kept his word. The soul who on Jesus had leaned for succor had not been forsaken. Jesus had leaned for succor had not been forsaken even in this terrible hour of massacre, and in their infamous extermination of the Mormons from Missouri in the years 1838–39.

One incident more, as a fitting close.

Over that rude grave—that well—where the nineteen martyrs slept, where my murdered husband and boy were entombed, the mobbers of Missouri, with an exquisite fiendishness which no savages could have conceived had constructed a rude privy. This they constantly used with a delight which demons might have envied, if demons are more wicked and horribly beastly than were they.

Thus ends my chapter of the Haun's Mill massacre, to ride in judgement against them!

It should be reinforced that Captain Comstock had lived in peace with the Mormons until pressure was put on him to lead the charge. Perhaps if the Mormons had not renewed their patrols, violating the treaty they'd just signed with Captain Comstock, he might have resisted the men who wanted to attack the settlement. In the face of the general unrest and violence throughout the countryside, the Mormons did not trust Captain Mann, who was marching towards them, and were afraid to completely trust Captain Comstock. Yet, it would seem that Comstock was the one who brought the food to Amanda and her children. He also stood aside and let her retrieve her two horses when he could have stopped her. Under the circumstances Captain Comstock appeared to have some empathy for Amanda's suffering.

5

Willard Gilbert Smith's Narration

In her terrible sorrow and bereavement,
her only help could come from a divine guidance.

W*illard Gilbert Smith, son of Warren and Amanda Barnes Smith and eldest of their five children, was born on May 9, 1827, in Amherst, Ohio. He joined the church in 1831 and traveled with his parents to Missouri with the Joseph Young party. After the Haun's Mill incident he moved to Nauvoo with his family and learned the trade of a stonecutter. In 1846 Smith joined the Mormon Battalion bound for California, finally arriving in Utah in 1848. In 1860 he went on a mission to England, and five years later he was ordained a bishop in Morgan, Utah. In 1877 he was the first stake president of the Morgan Stake. He died on November 21, 1903, in Logan, Utah, at the age of seventy-six.*

Smith was only eleven years old at the time of the Haun's Mill massacre. He found his father and brother, Sardius, dead in the blacksmith shop after the mob had gone. His other brother, Alma, was near death with his hip shot away. In his own words he tells how his mother cured the hip and found the courage to go on through her faith in her Heavenly Father.[1]

---

[1]The account is taken from a transcription by Dr. Alexander L. Baugh found in *Missouri Mormon Frontier Foundation Newsletter,* no. 18/19, Jackson County, Missouri. Interestingly, Professor Baugh states he came across it by chance in an obscure LDS family history and genealogy publication by the Fry family association: Jeanine Fry Ricketts, ed., *By Their Fruits: A History and Genealogy of the Fry Family of Wiltshire, England, and Their Descendants, Including the Allied Lines of Harwood, Ramsden, Toomer, Thurston, Bosen and Maddox* (Salt Lake City: n.p., n. d.), 181–83.

❁   ❁   ❁

With my two younger brothers, I was at the blacksmith shop with Father when without warning a large body of mounted men with faces blackened or painted like Indians rode up yelling and commenced shooting into the group. The men at the shop called for "quarters" but the mob paid no attention, continuing to shoot. The men then shouted to their wives to take the children and run for their lives.

We were surrounded on three sides by the mob, and the old mill and the millpond were on the other. The men ran for the shop, taking the little boys with them. My two little brothers ran with Father. But when I tried to enter the shop, my arms flew up and braced themselves against each side of the door, preventing my entrance. In my frenzy of fear, I again tried to enter the shop, and again my arms were braced to prevent my going in. After a third futile attempt, I ran around the corner of the shop and crawled into a pile of lumber, hiding as best I could.

Immediately, the mob began shooting at me and the splintered lumber flew all around. I crawled out and ran into an empty house on the slope near the pond. Here I found an old Revolutionary Soldier, Father McBride, who had been wounded and had crawled into a potato cellar under the floor of the house. Although I warned (him) that the mob would find and kill him, he begged for a drink of water and to be helped out of the cellar. I then went to the millpond to get him some water and was deliberately fired upon, the bullets spattering in the water like hail. I escaped without a scratch. (The mob did find this aged Veteran, and as he raised his hands in supplication for mercy, they were hacked and the fingers split down by a dull corn cutter.)

I made the old gentleman as comfortable as possible and as the bullets were flying thickly around us, I ran from this house into another one close by. Here I heard sobs and whispered comfortings, and lifting the valance around the bed, I found six little girls huddled in fear. As the bullets had followed me into this house, I said to the little girls: "Come we must get out of here or we will all be killed." So we ran to the millrace which we crossed on a board reaching the woods on the other wise of the pond with the mob shooting at us all the way.

After our race for life, the little girls scurried off like prairie chickens into the brush and tall corn. Knowing that my father and two brothers were in the shop with the mob still firing, I took shelter behind a large tree where I could watch the activities of the mob with comparative safety. Finally, they ceased firing, dismounted, and went into the shop where they finished killing any whom they thought were not dead. From there, they went into all the cabins and tents destroying or taking groceries and furnishings. Then after taking all the horses belonging to their victims, they rode off howling like Indians.

As soon as I was sure they had gone, I started for the shop and was the first person to enter this holocaust, stepping over the dead body of my Father in doing so. I looked around and found my Sardi[u]s dead with the entire top of his head shot away, and my brother Alma almost lifeless lying among a pile of dead where he had been thrown by the mobsters who, evidently, thought him dead. I picked up Alma from the dirt and was carrying him from the shop when I met my Mother who screamed: "They have killed my little Alma." I replied: "no mother, but Father and Sardis are dead." I begged her not to enter the shop but to help me with Alma.

Our tent had been looted, even the ticking cut and straw strewn about. Mother leveled the straw and covered it with some clothing and on this awful bed we placed Alma, cutting off his pants to determine the extent of his injury. After placing Alma on this improvised bed, my mother, Amanda Barnes Smith, a woman of dauntless courage and implicit faith in her Heavenly Father, found that the entire ball and socket of the left hip had been shot away leaving the bones about three or four inches apart. As soon as Alma was conscious, Mother asked him if he thought the Lord could make him another new hip, and he replied that if she thought he could, then he, too, believed it could be done. Then she called her remaining three children around the bed, and they knelt and supplicated the Lord for faith and guidance. Mother dedicated Alma to the Lord, praying that he be restored and made well and strong, but if this were not possible, to take him in his innocence. This picture of my Mother's implicit faith in her Heavenly Father remained as a living testimony to her children through their lives.

In her terrible sorrow and bereavement, her only help could come from divine guidance. By inspiration, her prayers were answered and she knew what to do. First she was directed to take the ashes from a fireplace and make a mild lye solution with which she bathed the gaping wound until it was as white as the breast of a chicken, with all the mangled flesh and bone gone. Then she prayed for further guidance and was prompted to take the roots from the slippery elm tree and made poultices for application. She asked me if I had seen any elm trees, and I replied that there were some on the banks of the stream feeding the millpond.

By this time, dark had descended upon this tragic scene, and when my Mother asked if I could take a shovel and get some of the roots, you can appreciate the terror which gripped my heart as an eleven-year old child. However, Mother assured me that the Lord would protect me and with a lighted torch of Shagbark Hickory, I began my search.

Women and children were lamenting loss of husbands,

fathers, and children; dogs were howling, and the cattle smelling fresh blood were bellowing, and no one could know how many mobocrats lurked in the menacing shadows. It required all the courage I could summon to take the shovel, and with the aid of a dim torch, follow the stream and secure the roots from which Mother made a soothing poultice. The story of the miraculous healing of Alma's hip has been related many times, but few realize the constant terror of the stricken family, unable to leave the State as Alma could not be moved because of his injured hip; yet they were repeatedly warned that if they did not leave, they would be killed.

They were forbidden to call the family together for prayers or even to pray vocally alone. This Godless silence, Mother said, she could not stand, so one day, she went down into a corn field and crawled into a shock of the corn which had been cut. After carefully ascertaining that no one was within hearing distance, she said she "Prayed till her soul felt satisfied." As she left the shock of corn, although there was no one in sight, she plainly heard a voice repeating these words:

> That soul who on Jesus hath leaned for repose
> I cannot I will not desert to it foes.
> That soul, 'though all hell should endeavor to shake,
> I'll never, no never, no never forsake.

From that moment Mother said she had no further fear of the mob, and she inspired us children with faith that if we conscientiously did right, the Lord would shelter us from harm. Although Alma lay in the same position for five weeks while the wound was healing, strength seemed to come to the limb suddenly. One day, when Mother was carrying a bucket of water from the spring, she was alarmed to hear the children screaming in the house. She rushed through the door to see them all running about the room with Alma in lead, crying "I'm well, Ma, I'm well!" Something had grown in to take the place of the missing ball and socket, and he was able to use the limb with no inconvenience. Although it was necessary in later years to pad the side of his trousers, he never suffered any pain or discomfort, although he filled a mission in the Sandwich Islands where he did a great deal of walking.

As soon as Alma was well enough that we could plan to leave Missouri, great difficulties presented themselves, one being that our horses had been confiscated by the mob. Finally, I went with Mother to Captain Comstock, leader of the mob, and she demanded the horses, one of which was in the field. He said we might have the animal by paying $5.00 for its feed bill. This Mother could not do as all her money had been stolen by the mob. I admired her courage when she walked out into the field and tying her apron around the horse's neck, led it home with no further objections.

❁   ❁   ❁

In his article containing this account, Alexander Baugh concludes by drawing attention to the young boy's heroism in helping six young girls reach safety, and in helping Mr. McBride when he could have gone into hiding instead.

Smith's description of the massacre adds a number of interesting details to the historical record. His several attempts to secure his personal safety amid a barrage of constant gunfire further substantiates additional Mormon accounts of the fact that the Missourians were bent on wholesale murder and intentionally fired at innocent women and children, not just the Mormon defenders. The fact that only two children lost their lives, and only one child and one woman were injured, is remarkable considering the random shooting that occurred.

Young Willard's heroism is especially noteworthy, particularly in the case of his efforts to assist Father McBride and the six young girls whom he helped reach safety. In recounting the incident with McBride, additional information is learned concerning what happened to him just prior to his death. McBride went into the blacksmith shop and was either wounded while inside, or while making an attempt to escape. During his flight, he made his way to a cabin where he secured temporary safety in a potato cellar, but due to the extent of his injury, could go no further. While trying to make his own way to safety, young Willard came upon the injured man. Parched with thirst, McBride requested a drink of water which Willard heroically provided. A short time after this incident, McBride was discovered and brutally killed.

Finally, Willard fully believed divine providence interceded in sparing his life as noted by his description of some invisible force that prevented him from entering the blacksmith shop. Considering the fact that of the thirty-five men and boys who can be identified as having entered the structure, only five escaped without being killed or suffering some degree of injury. Following the ordeal, he clearly recognized that had he gone into the shop, chances were, he would have been killed or severely wounded.

6

Interesting Bits and Pieces

What follows are a variety of snippets from multiple sources containing interesting facts and miscellaneous short items or journal excerpts about some of the participants in the massacre. This chapter will include those interesting bits and pieces.

❀   ❀   ❀

Rumors flying and multiplying, often without fact, or with facts grossly exaggerated, had Missourians afraid of Mormons. Needless to say, the Mormons were terrified of Missourians.[1]

Whether their alarm was justified or not, it is evident from Missouri county histories (like that of Audrain County which is much farther away . . .) that Missourians were alarmed by the actions and rhetoric of the Mormons. The two short pieces which follow are pertinent to the Haun's Mill events.

During the Mormon War[,] Livingston County, in Missouri, was not an idle spectator, but an active participant. No Mormons lived in the county, but the people sided with the Gentile population of Daviess and other counties, and demanded the expulsion or extermination of the "Jo. Smithites." Early in the beginning of the troubles in 1838, a numerously signed petition was sent from this county to the

---

[1]From the *History of Caldwell and Livingston Counties* (St. Louis: National Historical Company, 1886), 700–1.

Governor asking him to expel the Mormons from Caldwell and Daviess counties, and from the State. Mr. Adam Black bore the petition to His Excellency.

It was a force largely composed of Livingston county men, and led by the sheriff, Col. Wm. O. Jennings, that engaged in the massacre at Haun's Mill, which is fully mentioned elsewhere in this volume. . . . Capt. Nehemiah Comstock, who lived in Greene township, was also a prominent actor in this tragedy. Certain members of Comstock's company are yet living in this county.

There were about 200 militiamen under arms during the fall of 1838. These were led by Col. Jennings, and scouted through this and Daviess county chiefly, occasionally visiting Caldwell. Comstock's company was stationed at Haun's mill for some weeks after the surrender at Far West. While in this county the militia lived on their friends, and on themselves. Mr. James Leeper, whose father and brother were under Jennings, relates that he perfectly remembers cutting up his father's corn to feed the horses of the troopers

A considerable sum of money was subscribed and given to Sheriff Jennings as a war fund, to defray certain expenses. In June, 1840, he turned over to the county treasurer, by order of the county court, a balance of this fund, amounting to $14.13, which sum was afterwards ordered paid to a Mrs. Marters.

❀   ❀   ❀

The second short excerpt provides some background to the Mormon War and Livingston County, Missouri.[2]

The Indian wars, the "Big Neck" and "Black Hawk," served to retard the settling of Livingston County. After the Indian "fright" subsided and the county began settling, the

---

[2]From Livingston County Centennial Committee, *History of Caldwell and Livingston Counties*, 42.

first conflict in which the county had part was the so-called Mormon War in 1838. While no Mormons lived in this county, its citizens did not stand by idle. Money was subscribed and a force of men, composed largely of Livingston County inhabitants, under the direction of William O. Jennings, marched to Caldwell and Daviess Counties where they participated in activities to drive out the Mormons. Captain Nehemiah Comstock also had a company. After the trouble was over, Mr. Jennings returned $14.13, the balance of the subscribed money, to the county treasurer. Editor's Note: There were some extenuating circumstances that would have made both the families of Dick Weldon[,] who moved from Clay County to Caldwell County, then to Daviess County, and the family of W. O. Jennings feel especially strong that the Mormons were going to try, and probably would if allowed, take over the entire area. Designating a county in Missouri for them to live in would not keep them from spreading into adjoining counties.

The last sentence is a reference to the creation of Caldwell County, discussed in the introduction to this work.

❀   ❀   ❀

Hyrum Smith, brother of Joseph Smith, in his "statement" on record in the Family and Church History Department Archives, The Church of Jesus Christ of Latter-day Saints, Salt Lake City, Utah, makes the following reference to the affair at Haun's Mill.

Immediately after this there came into the city a messenger from Haun's Mill, bringing the intelligence of an awful massacre of the people who were residing in that place, and that a force of two hundred or three hundred detached from the main body of the army, under the superior command of Captain Nehemiah Comstock, who, the day previous, had promised them peace and protection, but on receiving a copy of the Governor's order to exterminate or to expel, from the hands of Colonel Ashley, he returned upon them the following day and surprised and massacred the whole population, and then came on to the town of Far West and entered into conjunction with the main body of the army. The messenger informed us that he himself with a few others fled into the thickets, which preserved them from massacre, and on the following morning returned and collected the dead bodies of the people and cast them into a well. There were upwards of twenty (?) who were dead or mortally wounded. One of the name of Yocum has lately had his leg amputated in consequence of wounds he then received. He had a ball shot through his head, which entered near his eye and came out the back part of his head, and another ball passed through one of his arms.

❀   ❀   ❀

The following is a copy of an article from the New Yorker *issue for December 1, 1838.*[3]

Further from the Mormons—The account of a bloody butchery of thirty-two Mormons, on Splawn's Creek, is fully confirmed. Two children were killed, we presume by accident: Considerable plunder—such as beds, hats, &c. were taken from the slaughtered. Not one of the assailants was killed or hurt.

About the time of the surrender, several Mormon houses were burnt in Chariton; and one Mormon who refused to leave, killed.

At Far West, after the surrender, a Mormon had his brains dashed out by a man who accused the Mormon of burning his house in Davies. (St. Louis Gaz. 10th inst.)

---

[3] *New Yorker*, December 1, 1838, p. 172.

We copy the above paragraphs from the Gazette of Saturday evening. We are sorry to say that our own information corroborates the details. For the honor of the State, we could have wished that such savage enormities had not attended a controversy in itself disgraceful enough. Splawn's creek, was not attached to any division of the army, but was fighting on its own hook. The men were principally from Charitou county, and amongst the number was at least one member of the Legislature. The enemy had approached within eighty yards of the Mormons before they were apprized of their approach. The Mormons had their families with them, and to preserve their lives, the men separated from them and took refuge in a blacksmith's shop. Here they were murdered? It is said that the Mormons had arms, but it is a little singular that they should have used them so ineffectually as not to have touched one of the assailants. The latter, in some instances, placed their guns between the logs of the house, and deliberately fired at the victims within. These reports are founded as they are, are not likely to be overcharged. Will the actors in the tragedy be suffered, by the Courts of that district, to go unpunished?

From all accounts, the children were not killed by accident. Sardius Smith, age ten, was deliberately shot point blank—with a recorded asswertion by the shooter that "Nits will make lice. . . ."

❀　　　❀　　　❀

An interesting paragraph containing the remarks of one of the Missourians, Daniel Ashby, follows.[4]

Attackers overwhelmed the defenders, closing into a tight half circle around the shop. Daniel Ashby, one of the regulators, moved in to secure the structure. He crawled over

---

[4] "Document Containing the Correspondence . . . ," *Boon's Lick Democrat*, 82–83.

under one of the openings from which the Mormons were shooting and within a short time, "our men got possession of all the port house, cracks, &c . . . and kept up such a constant fire that the Mormons could not get their guns out to shoot." Daniel Ashby to John B. Clark, 29 November 1838.

If there was any remorse from Ashby, it doesn't come across.

❀   ❀   ❀

Following is a brief excerpt about Oliver Walker.[5]

Oliver Walker was a Justice of the Peace in Randolph County, Indiana. His son John R. Walker and family were in Jackson County in 1833. John related that he was "driven out by the Hands of a mob who pillaged and destroyed my Goods &C. In Jackson and Caldwell Countys and Which Losses I Certify To be no Less than Five Hundred Dollars further that I suffered many Injuries from this mob By Breaking in my Windows by thrusting Long Poles Through at My family and Driving them from their Habitation."

Oliver and family were camped about five miles from Haun's Mill. He became very involved in efforts to avert an attack on the mill, making his home available for representatives of both parties to meet. *To no avail as it turned out, but he wanted to be a peace maker.* Oliver visited Haun's Mill to check on a member's welfare and was caught in the massacre. Orson F. Whitney in his *History of Utah*, vol. 4, p. 192, tells what happened to Oliver. "In the spring of 1838 the Walkers with several other families left Ogdensburg for Western Missouri, where they arrived just as the anti-Mormon troubles were at their height. While traveling through the State

---

[5]Gwilliam, "Oliver and Nancy Walker," http://www.farwesthistory.com /walker.htm, accessed May 2006. Oliver Walker was born in New York City in 1782. He married Nancy Cresse in 1803. They endured many of the persecutions of the Mormons. Oliver died in Nauvoo, Illinois, on April 13, 1843.

they were surrounded by an armed mob who searched their wagons, robbed them of their rifles and ammunition and warned them that they would be killed if they went any farther. Terrified by these threats two families stayed behind, while the others continued on to Shoal Creek, camping five miles below Haun's Mill. William's father visited that ill-starred settlement in quest of information as to the true state of affairs, and was there when Comstock's murderous ruffians fell upon the defenseless settlers and massacred nearly a score. Mr. Walker was wounded, and while hiding under some slabs that projected over or leaned against the bank of the creek near the mill, witnessed the brutal butchery of the revolutionary veteran, Father McBride, who, while pleading for mercy, was hacked to pieces by a stalwart Missourian with an old corn-cutter. Refugees from the mills reported the massacre to the campers on Shoal Creek, who supposed Mr. Walker to be among the slain. To their great joy they learned to the contrary after moving their camp about one hundred miles, when William sought and found his sire and brought him back to his family and friends. In November, while temporarily occupying a log house, the Walkers, father and son, assisted President Joseph Young and family, refugees from Haun's Mill, a distance of a hundred and fifty miles, on their way to Illinois."

Oliver's daughter, Evaline Walker, married James Henry Rollins on Shoal Creek, 4 miles from Haun's Mill just four days after the massacre there.

❖   ❖   ❖

The following excerpt from James H. Rollins recalls an interesting event in Far West, presumably before the massacre.[6]

---

[6]James Rollins, "Autobiography," BYU Special Collections, 7–8. It can also be accessed at http://www.ldshistory.net/pc/jhrauto.htm, accessed May 2006.

Col George M. Hinkle ordered 50 men to go and relieve or guard them, but only our 10 volunteered to go. We were determined to go and help our brethren. As we rode across the square, Joseph the Prophet came out of George Robertson's house, where David Patten and Obanion lay dead. He came out without hat or coat and stopped us, asking us where we were going. We told him we were going to Haun's Mill. He told us that we were his men and we must not go if we did go against his advice and council there would not be one (of) us left to tell the tale tomorrow morning. He was very pale and white. He said, "Go put up your horses and help us to bury these two brethren." And we did just as he told us.

❖   ❖   ❖

Another point of view comes from Jerold and Sandra Tanner in their article about Legacy, *a movie about the early days of the LDS Church.*[7]

The film "Legacy" shows an attack on the Mormons by the Missourians at Haun's Mill. According to Joseph Fielding Smith, who later became president of the church, seventeen people were killed. (*Essentials in Church History,* page 235.) Two of the victims were boys under ten years of age. Joseph Fielding Smith cited the *History of Caldwell County* which said that an old man was wounded in the attack and then "frightfully mangled." It was reported that he was mutilated with "a rude sword, or corn knife." (*Essentials in Church History,* page 235.) On the same page Smith spoke of "the diabolical deeds" of the members of the militia. He did, however, acknowledge on page 234 that "the executioners were principally seeking for the men, and let most of the women escape."

---

[7]This is taken from the *Salt Lake City Messenger,* no. 88 (May 1995).

There is, of course, no way that a person can justify this bloody deed. Dr. [Michael] Quinn was very disturbed by the "brutality of the anti-Mormon" militia that "attacked the LDS settlement at Haun's Mill," but he put the matter into perspective by showing that the action of the Danites at the Battle of Crooked River led to the slaughter at Haun's Mill.

❀   ❀   ❀

Pearl Wilcox tells of the happenings of three men for whom journals aren't available, or perhaps weren't written. Ms. Wilcox obtained this information from the Saints' Herald, *42: 676 and the* Saints' Herald, *45: 452.*[8]

Samuel Wood, when he first ran to the blacksmith shop, found the door barricaded.[9] He fled to the woods with bullets falling all around him, but he escaped injury.

Robert Rathbun and his son Hiram fled in the direction of the timber.[10] A bullet hit the young man in the thigh, and his father hastily put him on his back and carried him to the safety of the timber. From this wound young Hiram was a cripple for life. He must have been seventeen years old at the time.

Charley Merrick ran from the shop but did not get far until he received a load of buckshot and a rifle ball. He died in about five weeks.

---

[8]Wilcox, *The Latter Day Saints on the Missouri Frontier*, 258.

[9]Samuel Wood settled in western Iowa near Kanesvillle until the spring of 1851. He moved to Unionburg (Union Grove), Iowa, where he died in the faith on September 7, 1895.

[10]Hiram Rathbun was born on April 3, 1820, in Wayne County, Ohio. He was baptized and confirmed by Oliver Cowdery on November 20, 1831, on the Temple Lot in Independence, Missouri, before a large concourse of people. He was ordained at Haun's Mill on November 5, 1837, by his father, Robert Rathbun. He was an active minister until the martyrdom of Joseph and Hyrum Smith. The Rathbuns returned to Ohio, and Hiram taught school and studied medicine. He united with the Reorganized Church at Vassar, Michigan, on October 26, 1884. He was ordained an elder on November 3, 1884, at Galien, Michigan, and a high priest on April 10, 1891, at Kirtland. He died on May 13, 1898.

❋   ❋   ❋

Ms. Wilcox tells another interesting story that she secured from the Saints' Herald, *39: 445:*[11]

When the Rathbuns and the Brunsons[12] crossed the Mississippi River into Missouri en route to Haun's Mill, they were given a written notice which read: "You are hereby notified that all Mormons, or Latter day Saints, or those supposed to be Mormons, must leave the state of Missouri forthwith or are to be showed no quarters, favors, nor affections." Their wagons were searched but when they found nothing warlike, the Baptist elder-leader of the mob demanded to know their religion and then began to search for literature. Brother (Seymore) Brunson slipped his book of Mormon into the fire, and before it could be recovered it was beyond recognition. The Baptist preacher and the rest of the religionists were determined to have them all shot. This brought on a dispute, and they concluded to leave it to a vote. So while the religionists voted to kill them, a bare majority who professed no religion voted to let them go unharmed.

❋   ❋   ❋

A strange tale about B. F. Johnson[13] *comes from the* Millennial Star, *68: 43, or Lundwall,* The Fate of the Persecutors of Joseph

[11]Wilcox, *The Latter Day Saints on the Missouri Frontier,* 255.

[12]Seymore Brunson was born on September 18, 1799, in Virginia, the son of Reuben and Salley (Clark) Brunson. He served in the War of 1812. He was baptized in Ohio in 1831 by Solomon Hancock and was ordained an elder on January 21, 1831. He moved to Far West in 1837. On August 10, 1840, he died at Nauvoo, Illinois.

[13]Benjamin F. Johnson, son of Ezekiel Johnson and Julia Hills was born on July 28, 1818. He joined the church in 1835 and endured the hardships of the early persecutions, moving west with the Mormons and arriving in Salt Lake Valley on October 22, 1848. He lived a productive useful life, staying faithful to his children and leaving a large family, having helped colonize the West. He died on November 18, 1905, in Mesa, Arizona.

Smith, *p. 46.*[14] *B. F. Johnson wasn't in the massacre, but in the vicinity where he was captured.*

"Deny your faith or die," was the cry in the supposed land of liberty. Fleeing from Haun's Mill, Benjamin F. Johnson was taken prisoner and threatened day after day with the corn knife that was still dyed with McBride's blood. One brute pointed a rifle at Johnson's head, saying, "You give up Mormonism right now, or I'll shoot you."

Receiving a decisive refusal, the mob bully shouted with a fearful oath, "I'll send you to hell right now," took deliberate aim from about ten feet distant, and pulled the trigger. No explosion occurred. He cursed, saying that he had used the gun for twenty-five years and it had never misfired. He reloaded it for the third time with the same results, but finally on the last fire the gun burst and killed the man.

Johnson was liked by the commanding officer, who offered to adopt him if he would give up his religion. Since no argument would alter the young man's decision to hold fast to his beliefs, the general said: "Well, all I can do is to turn you loose in the woods, and let you escape if you can." Young Johnson was conducted to a deserted log house about one-half mile from camp, where he was left to make his escape.

These first pioneers of Fairview Township left, an example of loyalty to their chosen religion, a religion which they loved enough to live and die for.

❀   ❀   ❀

Ms. Wilcox offers her conclusion to these events:[15]

It cannot be denied that there were two sides to the Latter Day Saint problems in the state; but an impartial observ-

---

[14]Wilcox, *The Latter Day Saints on the Missouri Frontier,* 262.
[15]Wilcox, *The Latter Day Saints on the Missouri Frontier,* 328.

er, in the light of history, is forced to the conclusion that the expulsion of the Saints from the state was neither justified nor necessary and was a mistake of the gravest kind on the part of the authorities. If the Saints were the kind of people to require such drastic action, criminal and treasonable in character, it was not the part of good citizenship to inflict them on a neighbor state.

Doubtless the old citizens had much to complain of, for in that day on the frontier only a rough sense of justice obtained, and religion received scant attention. It was but a natural consequence that a sect laying such stress on their peculiar belief should come in contact with opposition.

❀   ❀   ❀

In 1839 John P. Greene, a Mormon and brother-in-law of Brigham Young, armed with documentation of the events of the Mormon War, traveled to Cincinnati, Ohio, and placed the plight of the Mormons before the citizens of that community. A notice was published in the Cincinnati Daily News, *June 18, 1839.*

Public Meeting
The Mormons

Mr. Green proposes, at Cincinnati, Ohio, to state to a public meeting, the story of the outrages and sufferings heaped upon the Mormons. Mr. Green is furnished with documentary evidence of what he proposes to state, and when he shall have satisfied his hearers of the justness of his story, he will appeal to them for contributions to relieve the wants and privations of women and children.

The minutes of the meeting appeared the next day in the New York American:[16]

Agreeably to public notice, a meeting was held in the College Chapel last evening, which was opened by a few

---

[16]*New York American*, June 27, 1839, p. 2.

remarks from a gentleman accompanying Mr. Green; after which Mr. Green gave a statement of the early settlement of the Mormons in Missouri, and a history of their persecution, which has hardly a parallel even in the persecution of the primitive Christians. They were ruthlessly driven from their homes, their property destroyed, the women and children forced into the woods, without any shelter from the inclemency of the weather, (it being in the month of January,) where they roamed about till their feet became so sore that their enemies tracked them by foot-prints of blood. The men were in many instances cruelly murdered.

On one occasion the mob attacked a smith-shop, into which nine of the Mormons and two boys had taken refuge; it being a log house, the mob fired between the logs, and killed every individual of the nine men: they then entered and dragged the two boys from under the bellows, who begged for mercy in most piteous tones, one of the miscreants applying his rifle to the ear of the youngest, (who was but nine years old, said) 'My lad, we have no time to quarter you, but we will have you,' and immediately shot away the whole upper portion of his head. The other boy was severely wounded in the hip, but had the presence of mind to fall and remain quiet, and so escaped: he is still living, and is at Quincy, Ill. Speaking of the massacre, he said, 'they had killed my father and brother, and I was afraid if I moved they would kill me too.'

To cap the climax, the villains plundered the dead bodies of their clothes, &c. In another instance, a part of the mob pursued an aged man, who, finding he could not escape, turned and raising his hands to Heaven, begged for mercy; the reply he received was a shot from a rifle, and he fell mortally wounded; he still besought them to spare him, when one of the party picked up a scythe, or sickle, and literally hacked him to pieces as he lay on the ground. This man assisted in the achievement of our liberties in the revolutionary war. Mr. Green's narrative contained many such instances, and was indeed a tale of woe and suffering, at which the heart sickens.

Hon. Thomas Morris then addressed the meeting. He said he had been in the vicinity of these transactions, and had taken some pains to acquaint himself with the facts: and from all he could learn, the Mormons were an industrious and harmless people, that no specific charges had been brought against them by the executive of Missouri, but that their persecution was for no other reason than that their religion gave offence to a mob—for causes which may at any time induce the same persecution of any religious sect in our land. He said he believed the statements made by the gentlemen to be true, and that they were corroborated by those who resided in the vicinity of their occurrence.

On motion, a chairman and secretary were appointed, and resolutions passed condemning the conduct of the executive of Missouri; appointing a committee to prepare a statement of the treatment received by this distressed people, and re-commending them to the favorable notice of the people of Cincinnati.

We hope the statement to be prepared by the Cincinnati Committee, will be as brief as it can be made, consistently with a full exposition of the facts, and that it will be circulated throughout the United States, and lead to some general plan for relief and indemnity—so far as indemnity can be afforded—to the survivors of these shocking and brutal persecutions. In this way only may we hope to redeem ourselves as a nation from the stain and the crime.

7

History of Austin and Nancy Elston Hammer

A crimson colored vapor, like a mist of thin cloud,
ascended up from the precise place where we knew the mill
to be located and was carried or streamed upward into the sky.

T*he following is related by John Hammer, who was nine years of age at the time of the Haun's Mill Massacre, and was the son of Austin and Nancy Elston Hammer.*[1] *I have included the aftermath from his journal due to its stark portrayal of the suffering of all of the* LDS *settlers as they were chased out of Missouri. In contrast to the wealth of material available about the emigration of the Saints to Salt Lake City, relatively little has been recorded about the terrible afflictions in the earlier years of the church.*[2]

❂   ❂   ❂

Austin Hammer (my father) was the son of John Hammer and Nancy York Hammer. He was born in the state of South

---

[1]Austin Hammer, the son of John and Nancy York Hammer, was born on May 6, 1804, in South Carolina. He married Nancy Elston on September 7, 1826, in Wayne County, Kentucky. She was born in February 1806, a daughter of Josiah Elston and Rebecca Lewis. Soon after their marriage they moved to Ohio, where they lived for three years. They then moved to Henry County, Indiana. After five years they moved to Shoal Creek, Caldwell County, Missouri, where they had title to 180 acres of land. Austin was killed on October 30, 1838, at Haun's Mill. Nancy Elston Hammer died at Smithfield, Cache County, Utah, on October 10, 1873.

[2]Littlefield, *Reminiscence of Latter Day Saints*, 66–76.

Carolina, May 6, 1804, and obeyed the gospel in 1835 in Henry County, state of Indiana. He moved to Clay County, Missouri, where he stayed a short time and soon after settled in Caldwell County, and made a cash entry of 120 acres of land and raised one crop of corn. His farm was within three or four miles of Haun's Mill, both situated on Shoal Creek.

In the fall of 1838, the mob threatened to burn this mill because it ground grain for the Mormons, and all the mills in that section of the country, controlled or owned by the mob party, refused to grind for them, hoping by so doing to starve the Mormons out. In consequence of these threats, a few of the brethren assisted in guarding the mill. This duty they had performed for several days and nights. The mob kept repeating their threats of violence. Finally some of our leading men interviewed the mob leaders who agreed upon a certain day when they would send a committee to the mill to confer with our brethren and see if terms could be agreed upon whereby a compromise could be arranged.

On the day thus fixed, being the 30th of October, a number of our brethren were at the mill hoping to have something of a reasonable talk, being of course, anxious that peace and security might be restored. With this understanding entered into, no violence from the mob party on that day was anticipated, and the brethren stacked their arms. The mob committee, however, did not make their appearance, but as the day was drawing to a close, a company of the mob, some two or three hundred strong, were seen partly sheltered from observation by the heavy timber nearby. Our brethren immediately hoisted a white flag. When the mob saw the flag, they knew they were discovered.

They rode rapidly on, led by Boregard and Comstock, and on their arrival at the mill one of them without saying a word to our men gave orders for their men to fire, which order was obeyed. Their leader then said to the brethren: "All who desire to save their lives and make peace run into the blacksmith shop," whereupon my father and my Uncle John York, together with others, ran into the shop, which was immediately surrounded by the infuriated assailants, who commenced firing between the logs, as there was no chinking between them. They also fired through a long opening made at one side of the shop by one of the logs having been sawed out to admit light and at the same time, they fired through the door which was standing open. Several were killed in the shop, my father being one of the number, seven balls being shot into his body, breaking both thigh bones. Some of the brethren thus shot down were dragged out into the yard so that their murderers might have a better chance and more room to strip them of their clothing. All who had on good coats and boots were rifled of these articles. My father had on a new pair of boots that fitted him tightly and in the efforts to get them off he was dragged and pulled out of the shop and about the yard in a barbarous manner. In his mangled condition, this cruel treatment must have caused him the most excruciating pain.

The brethren, seeing that the mob party were so numerous and bloodthirsty, concluded that it was useless to make any defense. Their only safety was in everyone making their escape the best way they could, which they did by fleeing into the woods and brush, or wherever they could secrete themselves. When the mob had murdered all they could find and robbed a number of their clothing, they retreated.

After the darkness of night had come on, the brethren who were in hiding began to make search for those who had been killed and wounded. My father was found and carried into Haun's house, where he died about 12 o'clock that night.

During that night they kept up the search as well as the darkness would permit, but were only able to find the wounded by their groans. All they were able in this manner to find were taken into Mr. Haun's house as soon as possible so as to be protected from being torn or mangled by the hogs with which the woods at that place were full. When daylight had fully come, the brethren who had been spared had to move with great caution, knowing that the mob was liable to fall upon them at any moment, for the purpose of finishing their bloody and damnable work.

Of course, there was no opportunity for affording the dead a decent and respectable burial. There was an old dry well nearby, and the only thing possible to be done was to place all the bodies of the dead into it. They were all put into this well together and the only burial clothes with which they could be clothed were just what this rapacious band of murderous vampires had left upon them. In this manner, seventeen bodies of our brethren found there their place of rest, my father and my uncle York being among the number. At the time of this sad occurrence, I was in the ninth year of my age.

I wish here to record a circumstance which occurred exactly at the time this blood deed was being enacted. I stood in the yard with my mother, my Aunt York, my cousin Isiah York and some of the smaller children of our two families. Our anxiety, of course, was great as to the fate of the brethren at Haun's Mill, knowing also that my father and Uncle had gone there to aid in its protection and assist those of our friends who lived there. We were standing there exactly at the time this bloody butchery was committed and of course, we were all looking eagerly in the direction of the mill. While in this attitude, a crimson colored vapor, like a mist or thin cloud, ascended up from the precise place where we knew the mill to be located and was carried or streamed upward into the sky, apparently as high as our sight could extend. This singular phenomenon like a transparent pillar of blood—remained there for a long time how long I am not now able correctly to state; but it was to be seen by us far into that fatal night, and according to my best recollection now, my mother's testimony was that it was to be seen there until morning. At that hour we had not heard a word of what had taken place at the mill; but as quick as my mother and aunt saw this red, blood-like token, they commenced to wring their hands and moan, declaring they knew that their husbands had been murdered.

Our uneasiness through that night was too great to be described, and when daylight came, my cousin rode to the mill in order to learn the facts in relation to what had taken place. On his arrival there, he learned concerning the massacre and brought us word back as soon as possible. The following morning my cousin and myself went to the mill and found that the dead had all been buried in the well by our brethren as before mentioned. We found the hat of my uncle York with a bullet hole made through it on the two sides at or near the place usually occupied by the band, showing that my uncle must have been shot through the head. We, at this time, went into the blacksmith shop previously spoken of, and there saw a sight truly appalling. The earth constituted the floor and in places where there were small hollows in the soil, the blood stood in pools from two to three inches deep. A boy had tried to hide by creeping under the bellows, but was discovered by the ruffians and killed. The boy begged piteously for his life, exclaiming, beseechingly, "Oh! Don't kill me, I am an American boy!" But this touching appeal to their patriotism was unheeded, and the innocent and noble boy while thus appealing to the memory of his native country had his brains dashed out which were plain to be seen upon the logs at the time of my visit.

As before stated, during the time of this bloody onslaught the brethren and sisters tried to save their lives by secreting themselves. One young lady by the name of Mary Stedwell secreted herself behind a large log. While in the act of hurriedly throwing herself behind this log, one of her hands received one of the enemy's bullets which passed through it at the palm.

The death of my father left our family in a very helpless and unprotected condition. It would have been an event sufficiently melancholy had he died of sickness, at home, where his family could have administered to his wants, and his last moments been soothed by those attentions which the hand of kindness and affection alone can satisfactorily administer. But to be cut down in his prime and torn thus suddenly and ruthlessly from wife and children so intensified the gloom which rested down upon our bereaved circle, that for a time it seemed that no ray of hope or joy would ever by able to penetrate our bosoms. And could we have been left, uninterrupted, to pass our season of grief that would have been a boon which we had not the privilege to enjoy. Those prowling fiends who like demons of hell had murdered the innocent and robbed them of their raiment, were still lurking around watching for new victims. Especially all the male members of the neighborhood had to keep concealed. The moment the mob got sight of them, they were shot at. The women were not quite so closely hunted and they, by being extremely cautious, managed to convey water and food to their husbands, sons and brothers, to keep them from famishing. Myself and cousin had to sleep in shocks of corn or in the brush for two or three weeks, not daring to enter the house, and we were kept from starving by the food which our mothers and sisters managed to convey to us. The nights were cold and frosty, which added seriously to our affliction.

After about three weeks from the time of the massacre, the mob sent our people word that we were all to leave that country inside of ten days or we would all be killed. They were doubtless stimulated to make this announcement because of the order of extermination which was issued by Governor Boggs. Whatever the cause was, it was equally cruel to be borne by our people. It affected our family equally with other members of the Church. The burden of all this preparation and removal, on our part, rested first upon my mother [Nancy Elson Hammer]. A less healthy and resolute woman could not have had the courage and endurance to grapple successfully with the obstacles that lay in her path. A family of six children upon her hands to be made ready for removal in ten days' time, would have been a wonderful undertaking in a time of peace with an abundance of means at her command. But she had neither peace or available means. True, my father left her 120 acres of excellent land, with a government title, a good crop of corn, already matured and ten or fifteen acres of fall wheat. But all this she had to leave for the enemy to appropriate to their own use. In fact all the comforts of home had to be sacrificed, and with the Saints of God, we had to flee, destitute and hunted, because of our religion.

The names of her children were Rebecca, Nancy, John, Josiah, Austin and Julian. My Mother's age at that time was about 32 years.

Well do I remember the sufferings and cruelties of those days. But we knew when the ten days were up that we would have to be on the move or our lives would be sacrificed. The Saints had no opportunity to sell their possessions, except in a few cases, and this is exactly what the mob wanted, knowing that they could take possession after they had compelled our removal.

Our family had one wagon, and one blind horse was all we possessed towards a team, and that one blind horse had to transport our effects to the state of Illinois. We traded our wagon with a brother who had two horses, for a light one horse wagon, thus accommodating both parties. Into this small wagon we placed our clothes, bedding, some corn meal and what scanty provisions we could muster, and started out into the cold and frost to travel on foot, to eat and sleep by the wayside with the canopy of heaven for a covering. But the biting frosts of those nights and the piercing winds were less barbarous and pitiful than the demons inhuman form before whose fury we fled.

The stars looked down upon us from the vaults of heaven, reminding us that God rules on high and took cognizance of the conditions of those who peopled His earth.

When night approached we would hunt for a log or fallen tree and if lucky enough to find one we would build fires by the sides of it. Those who had blankets or bedding camped down near enough to enjoy the warmth of the fire, which was kept burning through the entire night. Our family, as well as many others, were almost barefooted, and some had to wrap their feet in cloths in order to keep them from freezing and protect them from the sharp points of the frozen ground. This, at best, was very imperfect protection, and often the blood from our feet marked the frozen earth. My mother and sister were the only members of our family who had shoes, and these became worn out and almost useless before we reached the then hospitable shores of Illinois.

All of our family except the two youngest Austin and Julian had to walk every step of the entire distance, as our one horse was not able to haul a greater load; and that was a heavy burden for the poor animal. Everything bulky or anyway heavy was discarded before starting. Such articles as my father's cooperage tools, plows and farming implements we buried in the ground, where they may have remained undiscovered to the present time.

There was scarcely a day while we were on the road that it did not either snow or rain. The nights and mornings were very cold. Considering our unsheltered and exposed condition, it is a marvel with me to this day how we endured such fatigues without being disabled by sickness, if not death. But that merciful Being who "tempers the winds to the shorn lamb," sheltered and gave us courage, otherwise strength and our powers of endurance must have given way and we perished by the roadside. My mother seemed endowed with great fortitude and resolution, and appeared to be inspired to devise ways and plans whereby she could administer comforts to her suffering children and keep them in good spirits. Her faith and confidence had ever been great in the Lord; but now that all this care and responsibility came upon her shoulders, with no husband to lean upon, she felt indeed that God was her greatest and best friend, and she realized that He alone must be the deliverer of herself and family and conduct them to a people possessing the sympathies of humanity.

Yours truly,
John Hammer

8

Artemisia Sidnie Meyers

He told us to be faithful . . .

T*he following statement was taken from the Missouri Mormon Frontier Foundation and is in the Community of Christ Archives. Note the possible contradiction in the first part of this memoir as Ms. Myers states her father, Jacob Myers, "built a grist mill for Mr. Haun which afterwards was the scene of the massacre." A few lines later she says her "brother-in-law, James Houston, who was a blacksmith, built and owned the shop in which the massacre occurred."*

❖   ❖   ❖

I was born in Richland County Ohio on the 24th day of January 1829. My Father, Jacob Myers and my Mother Sarah Coleman Myers embraced the gospel about the year 1834 and moved to Missouri in 1836. They settled in the eastern part of Caldwell County near Shoal Creek, about 16 miles from Far West. He built a grist mill for Mr. Haun which afterwards was the scene of the massacre. I was baptized in the summer of 1837 when in my ninth year. In 1838 when the war broke out against the Saints, my brother Jacob Myers, Jr., was living near the mill and had been assisting in running it. My brother-in-law, James Houston, who was a blacksmith, built and owned the shop in which the massacre occurred. On the 30th of October 1838 most of the brethren living in the vicinity of Haun's Mill assembled there, among whom were my father and my brother George. My father with my brother-in-law accompanying him started for home before the mob came upon them at the mill. My brother-in-law's wife was at father's home. About dark word came to us that the mobbers were coming and that men, women and children had better hid[e] in the woods as they intended to kill all they could find. The men were told to hide by themselves. There were three families at father's house. After the men were gone the women took the children, and went about a mile and one-half to the woods. After the children were asleep and lights put out my mother put on a man's coat and stood guard until one or two o'clock, when word came to us they had had a battle at the mill and two of my brothers were wounded. We all then went home and found father there. Mother told him he had better stay with the children and she would go to the mill to see to my wounded brothers. I clung to my mother and wanted to go with her to which she consented. My brother George's wife also went with us. We lived three miles from the mill. My brother George lived one and a quarter miles from the mill. When we came to his house we found him lying on the bed. When Mother saw him she exclaimed: "Oh! Lord have mercy on my boy." He replied: "Don't fret Mother, I shall not die." He was very weak from the loss of blood. I will here relate the manner of his escape in his own words as he told us after he was better. "Our guns were in the blacksmith shop when the Mob came unexpectedly upon us. Orders were given to run to the shop. The mob formed a half circle on the north side of, the shop, extending partly across the east and west ends so as to cover all retreat from the shop. They commenced firing before we could escape with our arms. I looked for a chance to run out but as soon as I arose to run one fellow behind a tree leveled, his gun at me and I had to stop down again. One of the brethren by my side had just loaded his gun when he fell, mortally wounded. I seized his gun and raised my hat so that the mobber could see it immediately when he came around the tree so I could see him level his gun again at me, but I was too quick for him for when I fired he clasped his arms around the tree and slid to the ground. I now thought it was my time to escape. I made two or three jumps from the door when a bullet struck me a little below the right shoulder blade and lodged against the skin near the pit of my stomach. I fell to the ground, Mother, if ever a boy prayed I did at this time. I thought it would do me no good to lie there so I arose and ran up the hill, the bullets whistling by me all the time. When I came to the fence and was climbing over it, a ball passed through my shirt collar. I walked as far as I could but soon became so weak from loss of blood that I had to get on my hands and knees and crawl the rest of the way home. I was very thirsty, and finding no one at home, crawled to the spring and drank freely. When I got back to the house I became very sick and vomited a large quantity of blood. Then I felt more easy. I suffered terribly before this."

After Mother dressed George's wounds we went on to the mill where we arrived just at the break of day. I shall never forget the awful scene that met our eyes. When we first arrived at Haun's Mill the first scene that presented itself, in his dooryard, was the remains of father York and McBride and others covered with sheets. We went down the hill to cross the mill dam and there stood a boy over a pool of blood. He said: "Mother Myers this is the blood of my poor father." This, with the groans of the wounded, which we could distinctly hear, affected Mother so that she was unable to make any reply to the boy. We made our way to brother Jacob's house and found him with his left leg broken by a bullet about half way between his knee and ankle and a flesh wound in his thigh. After he fell to the ground the mobber saw him sitting there holding his leg and one of them ran up to him with a corn cutter to kill him. As he raised his arm to strike, another one of the mob called out to him and told him if he touched my brother he would shoot him. Running up to them he said my brother was a damned fine man for he had ground many a grist for him. After the mob had ceased firing my brother's wife and her sister saw him sitting where he had fallen. They went out and asked two of the mobbers to carry him into his house. The mobbers asked them if there were any Mormons in the house. They said there were not. They told the women that they would throw them into the millpond if they lied to them. They then took him up and carried him into his house and threw him on the bed, and hurried out of doors as though they expected to be shot the next moment. From my brother's house we went to the blacksmith shop where we beheld a most shocking sight. There lay the dead, the dying and the wounded, weltering in their blood where they fell. A young man, whose name was Simon Cox who lived with my Father, lay there with four bullets, having passed through his body the kidneys. He was still alive. He said to Mother. "All I want is a bowl of sweet milk and a feather bed to lie on." He had just got a pair of new boots a few days before and he told Mother how they dragged him about the shop to get them off. He told us to be faithful and said to me: "Be a good girl and obey your parents." He died in the afternoon about twenty-four hours after he was shot.

After we came back to my brother's house my Father, David Evans and Joseph Young, with one of two more came and gathered up the dead and carried them to my brother's

place, put the bodies (on) a wide board, and slid them off
feet foremost into a well which he had been digging but had
not yet come to water. Every time they brought one and slid
him in I screamed and cried. It was such an awful sight to
see them piled in the bottom in all shapes. After the dead
were buried (which was done in a great hurry), father and
the brethern went away and secreted themselves for fear the
mobbers would return. The mobbers returned, I do not
remember how soon, camping there about 20 days during
which time they killed cattle and hogs to live on. They also
took six or eight stands of bees belonging to Father which
were at the mill. During the time they camped there they
were very civil to the women folks. They chopped wood and
brought water for my brother's folks. They wanted to come
in the house and sit around the fire but Mother would not
allow them to do so. In the following spring my brothers had
so far recovered as to be able to go on board a streamer on
the Missouri River and return to Ohio where Jacob had to
have his leg amputated above the knee. George never became
a sound man again. Father moved his family in the spring of
1839 and settled near Payson, Adams County, and continued to live in that region till the exodus from Nauvoo.

*Interesting that a Missourian saved young Jacob's life, stating
he was a fine man who had ground many a grist for him.*

9

Nathan Kinsman Knight

*. . . shouting oaths that "if God did not
send all the Mormons to Hell, they would
take Jesus Christ and serve Him the same way."*

*Nathan Kinsman Knight was born on January 16, 1804,
in New England. He married Lois Witham and joined
the LDS church early in the 1830s, enduring the early persecutions of that group. He went with the Mormons to the Salt Lake
Valley in the spring of 1847. He raised a family and participated in
pioneering northern Utah. Nathan died in 1874 in Utah. His memoir follows.*[1]

❋   ❋   ❋

Nathan's own story: 17 August 1838. After being driven from
the state of Ohio, we traveled through Missouri along the
lower part of the state without any difficulty, the people
treating us kindly and advising us to leave the main road, as
mobs were collection [collecting] on it. We traveled on by
the roads and came out at the Grand River. Next day we
traveled across a prairie of thirty miles without inhabitant
and arrived at Whitney's Mill on Shoal Creek, Livingston
Co., Missouri. We crossed over the millpond next morning in a flat boat and started across to Caldwell County, a
distance of fourteen miles. When we were about two miles

---

[1] Knight, "Extracts from a Statement of Nathan K. Knight," 145–58.

on we met a party of sixty armed and mounted men led by Thomas O'Brien, who compelled us to give up our arms and return to Whitney Mill where we remained a week, waiting for the mob to determine whether to kill us or only take our property and drive us back out of the state.

Previous to returning to the mill they gave back my gun, as it was only a shotgun. While they were drunk and asleep one afternoon we hitched up, recrossed the Millpond, told the women living there that we were going back out of the state. We took the back track for two miles, where we halted a few minutes and requested Elder Joseph Young to take the lead of the company, which numbered eleven wagons and families. He objected but appointed Bro. Levi Merrick to take charge. We started everyone leaving the main road and taking a dividing ridge without any track and traveled on that afternoon and night and halted just before daybreak to bury a son of mine, fifteen years old who had died. At daybreak we started on again. In the middle of the afternoon we discovered a body of mounted men about two miles to our right, but a deep ravine prevented them from coming to us. They traveled on to the crossing of the Muddy three or four miles below, where they waited for us to come up and cross, but we kept straight on, crossed about two miles above them. Our teams seemed to take fresh courage and a drive of two and a half miles brought us to Bro. Walker's in Caldwell county without further interruption, where we fed our teams and animals, placed our wagons in position to defend ourselves, placed our women and children in the house and passed the night in peace.

The next day Bro. Walker's son-in-law piloted us to Haun's Mill, where we arrived in the afternoon. We found a number of brethren waiting to get their grinding done. We remained until the next morning and as we had been on short rations for a number of days we purchased some grain and as we could not get it ground until late in the day we concluded to wait until the next morning.

It was Tuesday October 30. The weather was pleasant the sun shining and clear. Children were playing on either side of the creek, mothers doing housework, fathers guarding the mill. 3:30 PM David Evans, Father Myers and another brother returned from an appointed meeting with the mob, who agreed in writing to let the saints alone if the saints would let them alone. Bro. Evans said he did not feel like the mob intended to keep their word and advised the brethren to keep out a double guard, and while he was organizing it and within half an hour after his return, his fears were confirmed, when he heard my daughter Mary cry out, "Look at the horses."

The mob led by John Comstock and numbering three hundred rushed out of the timber and hazel brush upon us. Mary carried Zalotis across the bridge where she cared for him.

The leader shouted, "Halt", and formed a line of battle, where upon they formed on his right and left making a half circle with Shoal Creek in front. The blacksmith shop was between us and the mill a distance of about six rods. I had just finished eating. I got my gun and hung my powder horn over my neck when the buckskin string was cut by a ball fired by their leader, which also passed through my breast pocket taking out my pocket knife. All fear left me at this time and I never had such presence of mind before or since. The brethren all ran in different directions some taking refuge in the Blacksmith shop. With the first shot, the leader shouted, "kill all! Spare none! Give no quarter." The women and children were so terrified that some of them would run in front of the mob's guns and cry "Murder! Murder!"

I took an active part in trying to get the women and children away and succeeded in helping about thirty to make
their escape across the creek and over the dam.

The war whoop and firing was kept up. By this time I was
closely hemmed in, some of the left wing had crossed the
Creek below the mill, where they attacked father McBride,
firing several balls into him and suahing [sawing?] upon him
with a corn cutter, striking him three blows before he fell
and a dozen of more after. They chopped him to death. I
tried to get to him but the men were between us. As one
man was running to help cut him down, swearing as he went.
I fired my gun, the first time. The ball passed thru one hip
and lodged in the other. He was always a cripple after. At
this junction I tried to escape thru the right wing.

At the Blacksmith shop they had killed Bro. Warren
Smith and one of his sons and wounded the other. The boys
were under the bellows pleading for their lives. The mob
put their guns thru between the logs and fired blowing the
top of one of the boys heads off and mangling the other's
thigh terribly. They shouted, "Kill them, damn them, kill
them. Knits make lice." Two men had Warren Smith
stripped of his coat and boots and were dragging him around
after he was dead and kicking him and shouting oaths that
"if God did not send all the Mormons to hell, they would
take Jesus Christ and serve Him the same way."

A number of the brethren were lying dead and wounded
near the blacksmith shop between there and the mill. I was
so completely hemmed in that I saw I had to fight my way
thru. When I could not use one end of my gun I used the
other. The first wound I received was in the finger of my
right hand. The next in my leg, the next in my body, the ball
entering just below the small of my back and lodging just
below the pit of my stomach. The last shot brought me onto

my hands and knees. I recovered myself and still stood in self-defense. I felt as though I had been pierced with a red-hot iron, and the blood soon filled my boots. I tried to escape across the mill dam by crossing the fore bay on a plank. Looking back I saw a man following my track. I turned and fired. He fell backward exclaiming, "O Lord Jesus have mercy on my poor soul." The contents of my gun had entered his bowels. He was a Methodist minister and captain of one company.

The mob now closed in around the mill pond, some crossing creek below to cut off my retreat. While crossing the dam and making my way along the edge of the pond to a dry ravine, a distance of ten rods, I was exposed to the incessant fire of the whole company, the balls flying passed like hail and completely riddling my pants and ball crowned beaver hat. There must have been from six to nine hundred shots fired at me as some of the party afterward declared that they all fired from two to three shots each.

I made my way up the ravine about one fourth of mile where I left my gun leaning against a Burr Oak tree, being so exhausted that I could not carry it further. I made out to get three fourths of a mile further through the timber and brush and secreted myself in some falled [fallen] trees. The mob must have followed me as far as my gun, for I never saw it afterwards, I remained there about three fourths of an hour. A little after sunset I saw Sister Polly Wood, formerly Miss Polly Merrill. I motioned for her to come to me, I could not call her neither could I stand up. She came and tried to lead me back but I was too weak. She kneeled down and placed her hands on my wounds and prayed the Lord to strengthen and heal me. The Lord answered her prayer and I received strength to walk back to the Haun's Mill, resting three or four times before reaching Bro. Hauns' house.

I had bled so much that my blood would hardly stain a white handkerchief.

I found my wife and part of my family, the rest did not come in until morning. The mob was all gone. The prophet Joseph in his journal said, "After the massacre was over, Bro. Knight heard Jesse Maupen say, 'He blew out the boys brains.'" Nothing had escaped the mobs ravage but Bro. Haun's house. Horses were taken. Just a small trunk left in the stable the contents gone all but a bottle of oil which was on the ground. Sister Haun and my wife passed the night in dressing the wounded and making comfortable as far as possible the wounded and dying.

The groans and shrieks made the night hideous and horrible beyond description and sister Haun and my wife were the only ones to administer comfort during the night of desolation and suffering. I prevailed on them to sing "Moroni's Lamentations" contained in our hymn book.

Early the next morning the men and women who had fled returned and as the murderers were expected to return and complete their work of death, no time was lost. The bodies of those murdered numbered seventeen. They were Warren Smith and his son Sardius, Thomas McBride, Benjamin Lewis, Levi N. Merrick, Alexander Campbell, Elias Benner, George S. Richards, Josiah Fuller, William Napier, Simon Cox, Augustine Harmer, Hyrum Abott, John Lee, John Byers, John York, Charles Merrick.

These bodies were placed in an unfinished well which had only been dug 14 to 15 feet deep. It had been made wider than a common well in order to admit a curb before walling it up with rock, as the ground was sandy. In this vault, wives assisted, placed their husbands and sons buried them hastily and fled again to the woods. I was removed to a log cabin near Haun's house, where I remained six weeks. The wounded that lay suffering along with myself were: Issac Laney, William Yokum, Jacob Myers, George Myers, Tarlton Lewis, Jacob Fontz [Foutz], Jacob Potts, Charles Jennison, John Walker, Alma Smith aged nine and his little sister.

A few days after the massacre the mob returned to the mill, ground up the brethren's grain in that region of the country. The mob now numbered one hundred. They remained about one month, killing hogs, robbing bee stands and hen houses. I and my family suffered much for food. Bishop Bingham and Brother Winslow Farr took their lives in their hands and brought my family to Far West.

I was compelled to remain at the mill for six weeks. During this time woman [women] milked cows and chopped the wood to keep warm. Winter was coming on cold and dreary. Spelling schools were held for the children and all were suffering alike as the wagons and tents had been robbed of clothing and bedding. The mob stripped the clothing from the dead, leaving them destitute of necessities of life.

At the end of the six weeks I began to get around he house a little and was again fired upon by a mob of fourteen men. I escaped into the woods unhurt. Alexander Williams came along with a pony which he had retaken from the mob. Which he put me on and we started for Far West. About midnight we passed a party of the mob. Their horses were tied to the fence and they were in the house drinking and carousing around.

10

The Story of Thomas McBride

*The bloody picture in the book of time, may it ever stamp
with stigma the brow of that government that offered
not a protecting hand to those who were ruthlessly
cut down—wounded, or were made widows,
and orphans, at the Haun's Mill Massacre.*

Thomas McBride's brutal murder was emblazoned on the memories of the survivors of Haun's Mill. McBride was born on March 12, 1776, in Bartley, Logan County, Virginia, the son of James McBride. About the year 1810 he removed to the town of Fairfield and thence to Wayne County. Here he served as justice of the peace for a number of years, and being converted to Mormonism, he was baptized about the year 1831 by Elder Hervey Green, but was never ordained to any office in the church. On the tenth day of June 1834, he crossed the Mississippi River into Missouri, where he lived two years in Bowling Green, Pike County, and after residing for a time in Ray County, he moved in 1836 to Caldwell County, Missouri, locating about a mile from Haun's Mill, where he was killed October 30, 1838. At the time of his death he was the acting justice of the peace for Grand River Township, Caldwell County, Missouri. Although some accounts state that McBride was a Revolutionary War veteran, his birth in 1776 makes it impossible.

This account was recorded by his by his son James, who survived the tragedy. Born May 9, 1818, James was baptized in June 1838 by David Evans. After the Haun's Mill massacre he moved his family to Nauvoo. In 1850 James joined the William Snow/Joseph Young Company emigrating to Utah, where he helped settle the *area of Tooele County. His birth year of 1818 would have made him twenty at the time of the massacre on October 30, 1838. Yet in his account James states he was twenty-five.*[1]

❀   ❀   ❀

In the spring of 1836, the company above mentioned, moved to Ray County, and there joined with a branch of the church. We stopped there about three months, during which time we suffered a great deal with ague [malaria] and fever.

The howling of the mob were heard on every side, and it was decided that we should move to Caldwell County.

In September, my father, taking with him what of his children yet remained at home, and accompanied by James Dayley and wife, moved to Caldwell County, and settled about three fourths of a mile from Haun's Mill on Shoal Creek.

There, my father entered from government eighty acres of land and began to make a home.

A branch of the church was organized at Haun's Mill, presided over by David Evans.

I was baptized into the Church of Jesus Christ of Latter-day Saints by David Evans, in June 1838. At the same time James [Jacob] Haun and Isaac Laney were baptized.

Though many of the followers of the Prophet Joseph Smith had been beaten, tarred and feathered, driven from their homes and their property confiscated for the use of mobocrats, their persecutions were not yet to cease. Threats were made against the Mormons, the rights of citizenship were denied them.

The little few now fully realizing the dangerous situation in which they were placed, decided to adopt measures to defend themselves against the raids of the mob. It was decided that a guard should be kept at the mill.

---

[1] James McBride, "Autobiography."

One beautiful afternoon on the 30th day of October 1838, my father came home from meeting with the brethren at the mill. He talked with me, and told me the arrangements made. He was called to help to form the guard. I was sick at the time, with the every-other-day ague, and father said on my well day, I should take his place with the guard and that he would guard on the day that I was sick. That with himself and me, he wished to fill one man's place. You will remember my father was then in his sixty-third year. During the summer he had been very sick—but having recovered, appeared to feel very well; in face I think he looked better than I had ever before saw him.

My sister Catherine was living at the mill with Haun's family. Leaving only me and my youngest sister Dorcas, at home with father and mother.

Father was in good spirits, and his countenance wore a cheerful expression. Having shaved himself in his usual style, leaving side beards—and taking with him his guns and blankets, started on his return to the mill to join the rest of the guard. Mother, with sister Dorcas started to visit a neighbor woman, living about a quarter of a mile distant from father's place. This being the day on which I was sick, the next day I should have taken father's place with the guard. I was then in my twenty-fifth year.

The day was gradually passing—evening was coming on.

The large red sun so characteristic of an Indian summer, shone through the smokey atmosphere. All was still.

My father had but little more than got to the mill—in fact not more than thirty minutes had elapsed from the time he left the house, when a gun was heard—and another—followed by the deadly crack of musketry, which told too well the fate of all who fell a prey to the blood-thirsty mob.

Perhaps not more than six minutes had passed from the

firing of the first gun, 'till the massacre was accomplished,—the bloody deed was done.

The firing ceased—the screams of mothers, daughters, and the wounded, told the dreadful tale!

The bloody picture in the book of time, may it ever stamp with stigma the brow of that government that offered not a protecting hand to those who were ruthlessly cut down—wounded, or were made widows, and orphans, at the Haun's Mill Massacre.

The sun slowly sank beneath the western horizon—and darkness spread its broad mantle over the universe.

With a single exception, the dead were left lying where they fell—in fact there were none left that were able to take care of them. Whether dead or alive, all feared alike—all was uncertain—all was pain and sorrow.

In vain did the affectionate wife with aching heart and streaming eyes watch through the long, long night for the return of her husband.

The 31st day dawned, and again the rays of the morning sun, kissed the landscape. As yet the extent of the massacre was not known.

Brother Amos having been detailed on the previous day to get wood for families, was on his way to the mill when he was told there had been serious trouble there. His home was about three miles from the mill, and as he was not detailed on guard, was not at the mill at the time of the slaughter.

He went on; and passing the mill a short distance, came to Haun's house. The first object that met his eye in human form, was the mangled body of my murdered father (Thomas McBride), lying in the door yard. He had been shot with his own gun, after having given it into the mobs possession. Was cut down and badly disfigured with a corn cutter, and left lying in the creek. Some of the women had dragged him from the creek into the door yard and left him there. One of his ears was almost cut from his head—deep gashes were cut in his shoulders; and some of his fingers cut till they would almost drop from his hand.

On further examination it was found that fifteen were murdered, and fifteen wounded—one of whom was a woman, Mary Stedwell, who in trying to escape, was shot through the hand, and fell behind a log. Several bullet holes were found in the log, directly opposite of where she lay. Alma Smith a small boy: and I believe one Merrick were the only wounded children that were yet alive. Of the wounded men, three afterward died. Making eighteen dead in all.

Isaac Laney a young man that was baptized into the church at the same time that I was, was in the black-smith shop, when the mob began to fire on them. His gun stock was shot to pieces in his hands. He then escaped from the shop, ran to the mill, and climbed down one of the mill timbers into the creek. That being the quickest way for him to escape danger. From there he went into the house, where sister Catherine, Mrs. Haun, Mrs. Merril and some other women were. They administered to Isaac, and put him under the floor. He had received eleven bullet marks in his body. I was well acquainted with Isaac Laney, and helped to take care of him until he recovered. He told me that when trying to escape from the mob, the blood gushing from his mouth would almost strangle him. While he was under the floor he said he suffered a great deal for want of water. The women not daring to venture out to get water until they felt sure the mob was entirely gone. Isaac recovered, and lived thirty-five years from the day of the Haun's Mill Massacre.

A few rods south of the blacksmith shop, was an unfinished well, about eight or twelve feet deep; but no water was in it. This made the sepulcher for the dead. Fifteen murdered persons, including my father, were carried on a board, one at a time, and dropped into that well—by brother Amos McBride, James Dayley and Jacob Myers; the only three able bodied men that were present.

It was not plainly shown that there was no mercy for us. What few men, and boys that were of much age—yet alive— were under necessity of hiding away, to escape danger.

About the first day of November, being tired of lying out in the woods, I concluded to venture a trip to the mill. I was anxious to see the grounds on which the slaughter took place; and learn if possible, the general situation of affairs. Accordingly, with feelings that I can not here describe, I slowly, wended my way to the spot. I walked over the grounds, noticing here and there the blood stained earth— and seriously reflecting on our then sorrowful situation. On the outside, the logs of the shop were defaced with bullet marks, and on the inside of the shop, the ground was scarcely visible for blood.

I traced the blood from the dead bodies of those who were carried and buried in the well. I went to the place and stood at the edge of the silent tomb of my beloved father. A silent prayer I offered to God and turned away.

I went to a house in which a widow woman lived, by name (William) Napier—her husband was a victim of the massacre. She was yet there with her family. She advised me to be careful least the mob might come upon me, and kill me.

Having spent a few minutes at the house, I went into the mill, to look once again through it. While there a noise attracted my attention, and I saw the woman of whom I have just spoken—running and beckoning to me in an affrighted manner. I sprang to the door-way, and saw about thirty rods distant a posse of men, coming in the direction of the mill. I did not feel right in trusting myself in their hands—

but rather than let them see me run to escape, I would have died. I therefore walked from the mill to the dam, crossed it, and quietly walked on until I was out of sight. Why they did not fire at me I can not tell.

A few days after, a company of men, commanded by Nehemiah Comstock took possession of the mill.

In that company was a man by name (Howard) Mopin, for whom, my father who was then a magistrate, had collected a judgment amounting to ten dollars and ten cents, just before his death. Mopin now threatened that my Mother's house would be burned down over us, if the money was not forth coming. I heard of the t[h]reats made, and after reflecting for a time took the money and started to chance my fate with the mob. In as bold a manner as I could assume, I went among them. They did not bother me, and I soon thought myself quite safe. I found Mopin, and presented him with the money. He took it, and seemed somewhat effected, on learning the situation of my father's family. To renumerate me for my trouble, he gave me ten cents.

I was quite small for my age—was smooth faced, and very sickly—which perhaps in part accounted for me being allowed to depart in peace. Having ventured thus far, I decided that I would again return, and act as a spy.

One day having worked my way back into their midst, I discovered that a man by name Robert White, who was a member of the Church [who] had turned traitor, and gave the enemy all the information he could about the Mormon families and their situations. The captain who was aside instructing his men, I overheard mention my brother Amos' name, as one having a gun—which he said was hid in a hollow tree. And if he refused to give it up when called for, they were instructed to shoot him down without further ceremony.

As soon as a chance presented itself, I left the camp, and as soon as I was out of their sight, made my way across the hills, to where Amos lived—and told him what I had heard. I advised him to go and get his gun, and demanded of him, to give it to them—as we were betrayed, and if he tried to keep his gun, he would lose his life. I then hurried away before the mob came. Amos done as I had advised him.

A few days after, brother Amos, James Dayley and David Lewis, were taken prisoners. They were kept a few days, harassed and tormented, and then set at liberty.

While Comstock's Company remained at the mill, they used it to do their grinding. They would shoot down our cattle and hogs—not caring how much they were needed by the widows and children that had been left to care for themselves. When they wished honey, they would take a hive to their camp, split it open with an ax, and help themselves. This was indeed hard to endure, but to resist was death.

The Governor of Missouri (Boggs) not being satisfied with the suffering already borne by the Latter-day Saints issued orders requiring them to surrender their fire arms, give up their principal leaders, and leave the state at a given time. The suffering caused by that exterminating order of Boggs', could hardly be described. Families were turned out of their homes, and the widows and orphans found themselves cast helplessly upon the mercy of the church. Some were without teams, and almost destitute of food and clothing. Thus exposed to the storms of winter, and travel a journey of more than two hundred miles.

It was now necessary to get rid of our home at the mill, in the best way we could. If we could get something for it, well and good, and if not, we were to leave it anyhow. The place was worth about one thousand dollars.

We left Haun's Mill, on the 24th of February, on our way to Illinois. The first day we traveled about nine miles—then camped in a house which had been vacated by one of the brethren. The day had turned extremely cold—and we decided to remain at tht place 'till the weather became more favorable for traveling. While there camped, we were informed that our guns, which had been taken from the saints at Haun's Mill, and at the surrender of arms at Far West, had been taken to Richmond in Ray County—and that we could get them by first describing them, swearing to the description—and paying a fee of sixty-cents for each gun. James Dayley and myself, decided to ascertain the truth of the matter, and if possible, get our guns. My main object was, however, to get possession of my father's gun—with which you may remember father was shot.

Accordingly about the 27th, we started to Richmond— at the same time, the main body of our company started on their journey to Illinois. We had no horses to ride—no teams were traveling in that direction—consequently, we were compelled to go on foot.

And now, let me say—this was the beginning of the three hardest days suffering from fatigue that I ever experienced.

11

Isaac Laney's Story

So bloody and shameful that I think its parallel
is not now on record even among savages.

T hree documents follow, two of which contain Isaac Laney's
account of the massacre, and one of which is a short biog-
raphical sketch by his grandson. In reading the account of
the wounds he suffered in the massacre, it seems impossible that
Isaac could have survived—but faith produces miracles. In the years
that followed, he went with the Mormons to Utah and lived a long
and useful life, dying on October 13, 1873.

❀   ❀   ❀

This first journal is copied from a photocopy of the original in the BYU
Library Special Collections. Spelling, wording, and punctuation are
not changed. A copy of it was contributed by Marilyn Richardson of
St. George, Utah, to the author of this book. Marilyn is Isaac's great-
granddaughter. She states the name is spelled Leaney in some records,
but the family prefers Laney. Extra space has been added at the end
of the sentences as it is evident no periods were used in the original.

while I was lieving near Hawns Mill on Shoal Creek Mo
and about the 25 or 26 of October 1838 I was informed that a
company of mob of seventy in number under Nahemiah
Cumstock had been to the mill and leveled pieces at those
present demanding all their guns   one man gave up his rifle
another who had his gun in hand refused and started off   two
of the mob followed and snaped their guns at him twice or

three times each   one of these men I was told was Hiram
Cumstock   the other name I never learned though the man
whom they were trying to shoot made his way off and gave
word to the neighbors who met the next day at the mill to
hear the story from the different families who informed us
that the mob had sworn the burning of the neighborhood and
mill with the other hard threats such as killing Hiram Abbot
who would not give up his gun   we also learned that there
was another company of men lying below us at house of mr.
Moe Crosby & knowing that either of those companies was
far superior to ours in number some of the neighbours wanted to leave their homes and run off but haveing only about
seven waggons to seventy three or four families we had to stay
and defend our selves and as I recollect it was on the twen-
tieighth of the month   we concluded to offer them terms of
peace but before our mesenger had started thare came one
from the company below us with a request that we would send
three men to the house of Oliver Walker to make a treaty with
three men which they would send to the same house   David
Evans Jacob Myers seignior and Anthonly [sic] Blackburn
was chosen to meet them   and on going to Walkers they
met ten men with each a rifle instead of three without arms
however peace prevailed and a treaty was soon made and
agreed upon   I suppose to the satisfaction of both sides
and on next day two of our men went back again   Those two
were Evans and Ames   they was told that the other company had sent a mesenger to Cumstock and his company with
word of the treaty between us and them   also told them that
we wanted to treat with them   they said that Cumstock
company was not only mad with us but mad with them for
making any kind of treaty with us   Evans sent them word
that he wanted nothing but peace and would not fight them
without offering them terms of peace   I cannot tell whether
or not they got the word or not but well I remember that on

the thirtyeth of October about three oclock in the afternoon Comstocks whole army of two hundred and fifty men came a pon us   Our company was about thirty seven in number being joined by a company of families traveling to the other side of that county and the adjoining counties stoped thare to get grinding at the mill   Comstocks company formed a kind of broken line at the distance of about seventy five yards situating their horses in front for a king of breastwork   commenced a fire without passing a word   Meantime Capt Evans advanced toward them and called aloud for quarters untill they fired   I sapose between fifty and a hundred rounds without any answer   then we could do no more than fire a few shots while the women and children made their escape afore the mob still advancing come within about four or five rods when I made my escape by flight being shot four times through the body and once across each arm being about the last man off the ground   now I am well aware that this is an incredible story to tell that one man being shot four times through body made his escape by flight but I have the scars to show   ten in number   one ball entering me through the inside corner of my left shoulder blade came out just about two and a half or three inches below my collar bone and as far as three inches on the right of the midle of my breast another entered through the muscle under the hind part of my left arm and passed through my body and came out under the middle of my right arm   another passed through my left hip on the inside or through the uper end of my hip bone another through my right hip   hit the bone just about the joint glanced out through the skin and rolled down my drawer leg in to my boot (note: he later told his son George C. H. Laney that he had one hit him in the back which he spit out of his mouth and this was the one that came closest to killing him.) [*This note inserted by one of the transcribers. Ed.*]   these four balls made eight visible wounds with two others   one

across each arm are all the wounds in my flesh I cannot tell
how many bullet holes was in my clothing   thare was twenty seven in my shirt   but to my story   haveing made my
own escape and hid myself I listened at them shooting the
wounded which could not escape   I was informed that one
of these murderers followed old father McBride in his retreat
and cut him down with an old sythe while he was pleading
for mercy   this was seen by Mrs. Ames and two other ladies
who were secreted under the creek bank   Waren Smith and
his son was also shot a second time   being unable to retreat
after their first wounds   Jacob Prouts and Wm Champlin
feined theirselves dead and lay still untill their pockets were
robed and after they supposed the wounded all were all dead
they robed the houses took the horses from the mill and* off
they went for the night   but on the first or second of Nov
they returned and camped at the mill robed that   plundered
the neighbourhood taking off such things as they pleased
Mob law being established

   *(I skipped a line . . . it should read . . . 'took the horses
from the mill and out of the stables and two waggons from
the mill and off they went for the night!') [*Inserted by a tran-
scriber. Ed.*]

   Those in this band of robers muderers and thieves was
Wm Man Esq   N. Cumstock Esq   Howard Maupin
Jesse Maupin   James and Shephard Reynolds   Callson
Runnels   Hiram Comstock   a young man named Glase
Erdsmans (or Erasmus) Sever   Jacob Rodgers   Robert
Write   George Millar   Sardi[u]s Smith   Elijah Prosper
(?)   these men came on painted black grimed of with red
rays and ribbons streaming like so many demons   enough
to disgrace a heathen forest much more a land of liberty
after some spent in this manner Captain went to Richmond
to draw pay for this service   I was told that instead of pay
they gave him a cursing and threatened him with justice

throwing the murder and robery in his teeth and orders to return the stolen property   this made Cumstock mad and on his way home he passed the mill and stuck up an addvertisement stating that the stolen property should be brought to his house and could be had by paying him for taking care of it   some of the property was got and I have seen some of the horses that was worked and rode nearly down   but some of the best of them could not be found for a small reward and one of the mob was going round trying to buy the chance of such they being about the best that was taken

The names of the murdered: Benjamine Lewis, John York, John Low, John Byers, Wm Napier, Warren Smith, Austin Hammer, Simon Cox, Levi Merick, Elias Benner, George Richards,   Campbell, Josiah Fuller, Thomas McBride, Sardis Smith a little boy
Wounded: Tarlton Lewis, Jacob Fouts, Jacob Myers, Jacob Haun, Jacob Potts, Isaac Leany, Wm Yocum, Nathan Night,   Walker, Charles Jamison, Alma Smith a little boy, Mary Steadwell, Hiram Abbot, Charles Merick a boy mortally wounded
This I will support in any court of Justice   April the 20 1839   Quincy Illinois
Isaac Laney

Isaac relates that the mob was painted in an awful way. It is not clear from his account when they were painted. It is doubtful that the militia members who participated in the massacre on October 30 were painted. It is probable that members of the mob, and possibly others, who came later were disguised in this manner.

❀   ❀   ❀

Another undated short statement was prepared by Isaac Laney. This appears to have been written at a later date, after he had had more time to ponder the massacre. His spelling and punctuation

have improved, but his great-granddaughter, Marilyn Richard-
son, says it is copied from his own handwritten copy. He also indents
his paragraphs. The spacing is his and he did use some punctuation.

In this account he is filled with anger, intense feeling, and dis-
appointment that such an incident could have happened in this
country.

Late this afternoon I was compelled to witness the massacre at Haun's Mill. So bloody and shameful that I think
its parallell is not now on record even among savages. In
open daylight in face of a solemn treaty and the most sacred
covenents, in free republican American in the state of Missouri an armed mob of near 300 men under peace officers of
the State and Ministers of the popular sects of the day invad-
ing an entire settlement, the lands bought of the General
government and occupied by unimpeached owners. But alas
the blood of male and female, old and young, the revolutionary soldier to the mere child was shed in torrents. After
even surrendering as prisioners, the dying were cut to pieces
and robbed of even the most ordinary clothing.

I scaped by flight shot four times clear through the body
and once across each arm, 27 bullet holes in my shirt, 12 in the
stock of my gun. [*line missing*] cut I bled till my blood would
not stain a white shirt. Was administered to by the sisters
and then by the brethern one of which said, "It was wrong
to flatter me as I must sureley die." "He said it was impossible for me to recover." I told him it did not hurt me and I
surely would get well.

My clothes being cut from wrist and from arms to the toes
of my boots on my feet. I was rolled out of them my wounds
washed & c.

Here the air was wrong [rung] with the cried [cries] of
orphans and widows who had come with fathers and husbands for safety. 17 being killed and as many more badly
wounded. Both cattle and dogs caught the scent of inno-

cent blood. I am sure the tongue of mortal could not describe the scene. Next day part of the mob returned boasted of the cruel murder and renewed the insults all they could.

I recovered, left Caldwell County Mar. 18th for Illinois.

❋   ❋   ❋

Further information was given in this unpublished biography, "Brief Sketch of the Life of Isaac Laney, by his grandson, George Culbert Laney." This transcript was also supplied by Marilyn Richardson. It gives interesting details that Isaac left out of his recitation. His family never believed a bullet went through his back and came out his mouth.

The 28th of October, 1838, found him with a small number of Saints working at a place called Hauns Mill, in Missouri. It was on this day that the mob came upon them demanding that they sign a treaty of peace and deliver up their weapons of war. The demand, of course, was outrageous and ridiculous, as they were minding their own business, making an honest living: however, they were allowed no word in the matter and had to comply. Grandfather had little faith in the mob's promise of peace. October 29, passed peacefully at the mill, but that night grandfather had a dream which was a warning to him. In the dream he seemed to be passing a trail where there were a great many snakes. They crawled along the ground, hurled themselves through the air and hung twisting and hissing from the limbs of trees. Dodge and hurry as he might, his body was soon pierced and bleeding from the attacks of the angry snakes. Finally escaping the serpents, he met a man with whom he was acquainted. "Brother Laney," he said, "you are terribly bitten and it is no use to encourage you, for no one was ever bitten as you are by snakes and live." "Well, then, I will be the first, for I am not going to die," was grandfather's answer. In a patriarchal blessing given to Grandfather Laney, he was told that he was a direct descendant of "Joseph, the Dreamer," son of Jacob, and that he inherited the gift of dreams. On October 30th, the mob, heavily armed, dashed down on the little party at the mill and began shooting. Grandfather gained possession of three guns, gave two of them to the other men and, placing himself between the mob and the cabin housing the women and children, began shooting. Lead was flying around like a hail storm. You may judge how thick was the hail of lead, for while he was preparing to shoot, eleven bullets hit the stock of his gun, cutting it off in his hands. One hit and knocked off the trigger guard, but the "works" were still intact, for he loaded and shot it once more and saw one of the mob drop as the result. Grandfather could see he was doing little good and they were cutting him to pieces, so he returned to the cabin, told the women and children to run for the woods. As he turned, a bullet struck him in the right arm-pit and came out of the left arm-pit. This was not the first wound he had received, for two bullets had passed through his breast and came out of his back, and two had passed through his hips from front to back. As he was running up the hill, his body much bent with effort, a large bullet struck him in the back near the kidneys, passing lengthwise through his body and came out of his mouth. This bullet he caught in his teeth and spit it out in his hand and placed it in his vest pocket as he ran. He said, "This one came nearer knocking me off my feet than any. The rest just 'plunked' through me as if I were a squash." Knowing he must hurry to help or give up his life, grandfather sat down to take off his boots; they were so heavy to lift in his weak condition. He had to slit his boots with his knife before he could remove them. Grandfather struggled on and soon met the man he had seen in the dream. He said, "Brother Laney, it is no use to encourage you for no man was ever shot as you are and lived," and grandfather replied, "Well, then, I will be the first one, for I am not going to die." Just a little farther on was the home of a friend who took him in and after washing and dressing his wounds, put him in bed. His clothes were cut to pieces and his body had been hit with seven bullets, leaving thirteen scars. For some time he lay near death, being fed with a spoon; he was so weak; he could not open or close his eyes. The elders were called in and he was anointed and promised in the name of Jesus Christ that he would recover. From this time on he rapidly recovered.

12

Ellis and Olive Eames

When I call this scene to mind it makes my poor old heart ache.

T he accounts of Ellis and Olive Gibbs Eames provide additional details concerning the massacre. Research reveals
that Olive Ames, as her name is given in the first account,
is actually Olive Eames. Her husband, Ellis Eames, is for an
unknown reason incorrectly listed in various accounts as Ellis
Eamut. Olive and her husband later moved to California, where
she died on December 2, 1900.

❄   ❄   ❄

*The account that follows is from the "Journal of Olive Ames
[Eames], a Survivor of the Haun's Mill Massacre."[1] It was written in October 1896, while she resided in San Bernardino, California.*

This dreadful massacre occurred October 30, 1838. There
was quite a settlement of saints at Haun's mill, there being
some dozen families or more. We had been living there a
year or so prior to the cruel treatment the saints received
during this massacre.

People came from far and near to the mill for the purpose
of getting their wheat and corn ground. We were living in
peace and quiet when word reached our ears that a mob was

---

[1]Smith III, *History of the Reorganized Church*, vol. 2, ch. 13. The account is also
included in Livingston County Centennial Committee, *History of Caldwell and
Livingston Counties, Missouri.*

coming to destroy Haun's mill. There being some thirty men of the brethren, they began immediately to make arrangements as to what would be best to do, so a few of the brethren went to Far West to seek assistance, and found they would be able to get some help if needed. But lo! One evening while I was busily engaged getting supper, and two of the brethren, Mr. Rial Ames (my husband's brother) and Hyrum Abbott were sitting just outside the door, one cutting the other's hair, they rose from the chair and remarked, "I see some of the brethren coming from Far West," when suddenly the party that was approaching began firing. Then said Mr. Ames, "It's the mob right on us. " The party consisted of two hundred men.

When I call this scene to mind it makes my poor old heart ache. Men, women, and poor little children running in every direction, not knowing what minute their lives would be taken. The mob continued firing, shooting at anyone they could see amidst the smoke. I rushed out of the house, crying, "Where are my children?" They gathered around me, then, with my babe, but one month old, in my arms, I started to hide, not knowing where to go or what to do, so frightened was I, but anxious to conceal my little ones somewhere. I soon found myself and little ones hidden away down under the bluff in a little nook by the creek. No sooner had I concealed myself there than my husband, Mr. Ames, and old Father McBride ran past hunting a place of concealment. He called to me as he passed, "Have you all the children?" "Yes," said I, "all four." As Rial Ames fled he remarked, "I guess Ellis's folks (that is myself and husband) are all murdered."

Isaac Laney crossed the creek above me. The mob saw him and began firing. I saw him fall, then rise and climb the hill. He escaped death, but carried a great many wounds. How he suffered that night!

Poor old Father McBride was overtaken by one of the mob, who took his gun, and not then being satisfied, he took a corn knife and hacked the poor old man on the head, then turned back to his company. As he passed my place of concealment I was crying, talking, and feeling oh! So dreadful after seeing such a dreadful sight as these two. He remarked to me while passing, "Don't be scared; you shan't be hurt."

By this time the firing ceased and they went to plundering. I came out from my place of concealment, crossed the creek, and went to Mrs. Haun's finding there women crying, heart broken, their husbands killed; others, their innocent little children were missing. Not knowing my husband's whereabouts, I was much worried; but word soon came saying he was safe.

While at Mrs. Haun's I could see them go into the houses and tents, carrying out clothing and bedding, etc. and pile it on Mr. Ames' horse, then they led him off. Of course money was what they were hunting for. What little money we had was hid away in my old clock. I supposed that too would be taken, with all my bedding.

Such a dreadful night we spent! Men, women, and children lying here, and there. Such mourning for their dear ones! Everything was in an uproar. Words cannot describe the awful scene. The wounded were numerous. Some were groaning; others we would refresh by moistening their mouths with a little cold water. It was an awful sad time.

The brethren came home in the night and buried the dead in the old well and cared for the wounded as best they could. During the night I persuaded a lady to go over home with me, as I was anxious to see if my money was safe in the old clock. Sure enough, there it was, but everything had been turned upside down and things carried off. We returned again to Mrs. Haun's and remained until morning.

On returning home next morning it was with heavy hearts we stepped in our doors, not knowing when the same scenes would be repeated. The sound of a horn was a signal they were coming.

After two days they again returned painted like Indians, and took possession of the mill. They had two prisoners with them. Part of the mob gathered the crops while others did the grinding, and then they sent the product home to their families, while we had to do without. They kept possession nine days, until they had stripped the fields. We had a number of hogs. They killed nine of ours while there. During their stay we were visited with a heavy snowstorm; soon after this they left. We took possession of the mill. (This mill was purchased by Mr. Haun and Mr. Ames from a Mr. Myers.) During their stay the brethren were all hid away.

A few months after this I went to Far West to visit Mother. She, too, was undergoing her share of trouble.

Father was put in jail at Richmond. Mother ground her buckwheat in a coffee mill to make bread. After a short visit I returned home, where we remained until next spring. During the winter we underwent a great many hardships. Abbey Ames (my stepdaughter) remained with me all winter. She was six years old the day that fearful massacre happened. She is now living in Los Angeles.

In the spring we began moving from one place to another, until we finally settled at Nauvoo.

I was born February 13, 1815, at Rutland, Rutland County, Vermont, and am now living in San Bernardino, California.

Olive Ames

I would like to mention about the cap my husband had on that day. He was a great hand to go hunting, so I made a cap for him and he happened to have it on that day. That saved him from being killed, so we thought after we talked it over. The mob thought he was one of them because of the red stripes in his cap. But there was a bullet hole in his coat tail. O. A.

It was interesting that Olive mentioned the men came back two days later dressed like Indians. The victims knew who the perpetrators were, so why the attempted disguise?

❂　　　❂　　　❂

Ellis Eames was born on January 19, 1809, in Mentor, Geagua County, Ohio. He married Olive Jane Gibbs around 1835. Following the Haun's Mill massacre, they moved to Nauvoo and then on to Utah in 1850. He helped colonize for a short time in Utah, was the first mayor of Provo, Utah, and then moved to San Bernardino in 1852, staying in California until he died on October 12, 1882. He was an accomplished fiddler. He and Olive joined the Reorganized Church of Jesus Christ of Latter-day Saints. The account that follows was ascribed to Ellis Eamut (actually Ellis Eames) and was transcribed at the Church Historian's Library in Salt Lake City from the Journal History of [LDS] Church (*October 30, 1838*): *11–16. More detail prior to the massacre has been included.*

On the 15th day of August, 1837, I moved from Far West to Haun's Mill, 16 miles from the former place, with a quantity of merchandise intending to keep store in that place; having settled there, and liking the country very much, I purchased a saw mill from Mr. Myers, and in the spring Mr. Myers and son and I built a grist mill which was furnished that season. All things continued to move on well, the inhabitants behaved themselves very friendly and purchased goods from and used my mill for grinding and sawing. This continued until the disturbances broke out in Daviess County, when I observed from the conversation that they did not like the proceedings of our brethren. However, they seemed to be kind as usual to me and the rest of our people, who were in the immediate neighborhood.

As the disturbances increased, and the excitement prevailed they partook of the same spirit and some threats were made by them of burning the mills. Three men, viz. Lardus Smith, George Miller, Robert White (one once a member of the Church) and the other two men left the place to move up to the Grand River. Thinking they would be protected in that place from the mob whom they feared would soon fall upon the brethren who were settled in Caldwell, these men who had left nearly all their property behind them agreed with the inhabitants amongst whom they had gone to reside to give them half of their stock, if they would drive it home for them.

Accordingly, about eighteen or twenty came for that purpose, but did not content themselves with driving off the property of the individuals, but likewise drove off two cows belonging to Gilman Merrick and several young stock from me. At the time they were coming they met a man by the name of Miller who was on horseback; they took his horse from him.

A few days after this Mr. Isaac Calkin had a beautiful span of horses which he secreted in the corn field, for fear the mob would steal them, but notwithstanding this precaution they succeeded in finding them and took them away.

The next important transaction that took place was that a company was raised on Grand River, but without any legal authority whatever and came to our neighborhood and took a quantity of guns from our people. When they came up to my place I immediately went up to them, conversed with them and asked what was their object in the strange move they were making. One of them named, Molsey, told me that they were taking the guns from the Mormons, wanting to put a stop to the damned fuss. One young man named Hiram Abbot who was with me, and with him I was about making arrangements to put up a store, who had a gun with him was told to give up his gun, but he refused, knowing they had no authority for such strange proceedings when several of the mob while on their horses immediately cocked their guns and took aim at him, but did not fire.

Three of them then dismounted vis: Hiram Cumstock, Trosher, and Whitney and pursued after him across the mill dam—he got up to the side of a hill and Cumstock got by the side of the house, Comstock then drew up his gun and snapped it three times at him, but without effect; his gun would not make fire. Abbott seeing that, cocked his gun, but Comstock got behind the hen house and screened himself from danger. Abbott then made his escape as fast as possible. The mob then rode off. Very soon after it was reported that they intended to come and burn the mills. On receiving this intelligence the neighbors assembled together to consult what was best to be done and after some deliberations it was agreed that there should a few remain at the mill to guard it from the attack of any individuals who might feel disposed to put their threats into execution, and from that time there were generally some of the men about the mills in order to protect it, it being their chief and only place where they could get any flour or meal.

The mob understanding that we had made such a movement, sent word to us that they wished to meet a committee of our people and have an understanding of each other's movements and expressed their wish to live in peace and friendly terms with us We immediately sent a committee who met them at the house of Mr. Myers, and after a short interview and explaining to them the object we had in view and that we desired to live in peace, and they separated both parties seemed satisfied and manifested a kind spirit. The committee on the part of the mob were Samuel S. Toss, Paceriah Lee, Isaac McCaskie, Thos. R. Brien, Clerk of the Circuit Court at Livingston, and William F. Ewe., Esq. The names of our brethren were David Evans, Jacob Myers and Anthony Blackburn. After this interview we felt more satisfied, having, as we thought, a perfect understanding of their intentions, but at the same time we thought it best to keep up a watch at the mills—for fear any individuals might come privately and burn them.

About this time a number of movers from the East came up, intending to settle in that section of the country, but had not determined where. They stopped a few days at the mills and purchased some provisions until they should find a place to settle.

We continued to hear of mobs in different directions, but at the same time we felt ourselves measurable safe after being given to understand by the committee from Capt. Mattison's company that they would not molest us, if we were peaceable, etc.

On the 31st of October things moved on as usual, we were occupied in our usual occupations and heard of nothing to increase our fears and were in hopes that soon such proceedings and alarm would cease and we should again enjoy the blessings of liberty and peace. The day was far spent; the sun was sinking fast in the western hemisphere, being only about an hour and a half high. A number of us were at a short distance from the mill between it and the blacksmith's shop when one observed there was a mob coming, and immediately we saw a large company of between 200 and 250 within about one hundred yards from us. Thinking their movements were hostile, we immediately ran into the blacksmith's shop, for safety. Some of our brethren had camped a little behind the shop; one of them by the name of Knight, had just taken up his gun and was going down to the small lake for the purpose of shooting ducks when the mob came upon him. One of their leaders named Comstock observing him immediately fired upon him and shot the strap off his shot pouch. He then ran into the shop whither we had taken shelter, the mob then kept rushing on towards the shop and shooting at us. David Evans then ran out and called for peace and solicited them to desist. Knight also went out again and joined him supplicating for peace, but all to no effect; they continued to fire upon them and shot Brother Knight in the hand, taking off one finger and disabling another, he then retreated towards the mill to cross on the dam, when he was shot in the back, the ball lodging in the pit of his stomach.

The women seeing our situation and expecting no better treatment took to flight, taking their little ones along with them and running away from a scene of murder, which it is impossible to portray. As the mob approached nearer the shop, (indeed if had all been armed it would have been impossible for us to have resisted them) took deliberate aim through the cracks and the shop being crowded almost every ball that entered the shop took effect and every moment someone was exclaiming, "Oh, I am shot," and first one and then another kept sinking down upon the ground, writhing in agony, while the blood flowed from their wounds and steamed upon the floor. One young man standing immediately next to me was shot, seeing no prospect before us but death, the mob manifesting all malice possible, and would not listen to our cries, and seemed determined to murder us all, we thought it advisable for us to try to make our escape by running out of the shop and cross the mill dam. Those of us who were able ran out and endeavored to make our escape in doing which as many were shot down while making the attempt and the mob firing upon us all the time as long as we were within reach. The mob then rushed into the shop where the wounded and dying were laying and those in whom the spark of life was not extinct were then shot over again. A little boy about nine years old who had hid himself under the bellows being observed and on being threatened to be shot, he earnestly desired and prayed for them to spare him, plead for his life, but to no purpose, for a muzzle shot gun was placed to his head and his brains were literally blown out, another little boy was likewise shot and died soon after, still another was shot, but has survived. One old gentleman who was immediately behind, named Thos. McBride, Esq., ran when we fled from the shop and was pursued, having a gun in his hand. This was demanded by his pursuer, he immediately turned round and delivered it up. The monster then took a corn cutter which he had by his side and cut the old man into pieces.

Some of the women were shot. Mrs. Merril's clothes were cut in two or three places with bullets and a young woman named Mary Studwell who was running away, at a distance from any one else was shot through the hand. Hearing the balls whistling by her she took shelter behind some logs which screened her from the balls as several lodged in the logs.

After they had finished their bloody work, the mob next commenced to plunder, and seeing some teams standing by belonging to the movers who had lately come along, they loaded the wagons with our goods. They entirely stripped me of all my clothing as well as my wife's and the clothes belonging to a young man who was boarding at our house, and all our bed clothes and beds likewise a quantity of merchandise which they carried away. Nor did this satisfy them, but those who were murdered were then robbed of their clothes, watches and everything else of value. The mobbers took their booty to Grand River and there made a distribution of the spoils amongst themselves.

I went about two miles and hid in the Hazel brush and then returned with Mr. Blackburn about ten O'clock at night. I went amongst my friends who had been shot and those who had been wounded, I assisted all I could and administered to their necessities, and early in the morning a few of us got together and interred the dead in a hole which had been dug for a well, and then we went and hid in the hazel brush, expecting the mob would probably be coming to massacre the remainder. Some came but they did not appear so hostile, but satisfied themselves with carrying off 2 or 3 horses. A few days after the same company came and pretended that General Clark had sent them to take prisoners and send them to Richmond jail. They took me prisoner and kept me in close confinement for nine days and would not let me converse with anyone. They then took possession of my mills and ground up all the wheat and corn and took it home to their families and after taking about all the spoil they could and killed nearly all my hogs, they departed and left me at liberty and drove off the cattle, etc. They went all around the neighborhood and threatened the lives of all those Mormons and ordered them out of the state upon pain of extermination. The names of those who were killed were as follows: Elias Benner, Josiah Fuller, John Boyers, from Ohio, Richland County, Simon Cox, George Richards, Thos. McBride, Levi McMerrick, John York, Austin Hammer, Warren Smith, Benjamin Lewis, Hiram Abbott, John Lee, Sardius Smith, Wm Roper and Merrill.

Wounded Elimar Merrill, Isaac Laney, William Yokum, Jacob Hammer, Jacob Foutz, George Meyers, Jacob Meyers, Jun., Jacob Potts, Charles Jameson, Carleton, Lewis.

The names of the leading characters who took part in this

outrage and inhuman butchery were as follows: Nehemiah Comstock, John Conmer,— Gee, Jennings, Sheriff of Livingston County, etc.

These acted without any authority and committed all these murders, and robberies, yet none of them have been brought to punishment. The affair was left without investigation and the poor afflicted broken-hearted survivors left without any redress.

13

David Lewis

Lord, Thou has delivered me for some purpose, and
I am willing to fulfill that purpose whenever
Thou makes it known unto me.

David Lewis was born on April 10, 1814, and died on September 2, 1855, in Parowan, Utah. David followed the Mormons to Nauvoo after the Haun's Mill massacre and emigrated to Utah, where he helped colonize the southern part of the territory. Three Lewis brothers, converts to the LDS Church, were at Haun's Mill. This account of David Lewis is a family record provided by Kathie Workman Moore, a great-great-granddaughter of David Lewis.

❊   ❊   ❊

I will now proceed to give an account of the massacre at Hawn's Mill, and the circumstance connected with it.

The people living on grand river about six or eight miles north of the mill began to come over to School [Shoal] Creek settlements where the mormons lived and drove off a drove of our cattle and made some threats that they intended to come and burn down the mill. We then sent delegates to them to see if we could not compromise with them and live in peace. They met our delegates with guns and in a hostile manner, but finally they agreed with our men that they wold be at pece with us. We had mostly gathered to the mill awaiting to hear from our delegates and to organize ourselves so that if they should come in a hostile manner we might be the better prepared to defend ourselves, for about thirty of them had come and taken the guns of all those that lived at the mill before, except Hyrum Abots who would not give his up although they had snapped there guns at him several times. There were also several brethren stopped at the mill that was just moving to that country from the eastern states, amongst whom was Joseph Young, the present president over the Seventy's and a brother of Brigham Young, the president of the Church. There were several tented in the mill yard with wagons and horses and all their substance, and there we were intermixed with women and children, there being about thirty men with guns only.

We were in no state of defence for we were not expecting, only that they would abide the treaty we had made with them and felt as if we were safe, although we had been counciled by Joseph the Prophet to leave the mill and go to Far West. We were deceived by the messenger we sent to him for council. We understood it not, for our messenger said to Joseph, "What shall we do that is at the mill"? Joseph said, "Gather up all of you and come to Far West." "What?" said the messenger, his name was Jacob Hawn, the owner of the mill, "Leave the mill and let it be burnt down, we think that we can maintain it." "If you maintain it," said Joseph, "you will do well—do as you please." The messenger returned and said if we thought we could maintain the mill it was Joseph's council for us to do so. If we thought not, to come to Far West. We thought, from the way the thing was represented it would be like cowards to leave and not try to maintain it, and as they had agreed to be at peace, we thought to gather up all our effects and leave our houses, would be useless, for we did not know that it was Joseph's council for us to do so.

While thus situated, on Tuesday, the 30th day of October, 1838, about three hundred armed men on horseback came in full lope towards us, until they got in about one hundred yards of us. They immediately halted and commenced firing at us.

At there first appearance, we did not know but they were brethren of the church, and did not try to place ourselves in a situation to defend ourselves, but soon we found them to be a hostile foe, deprived of all humanity or mercy for man. Our people cried out for mercy with uplifted hands when they were immediately shot down.

David Evans was our captain—he cried out for quarters, they gave none and he immediately fled, giving no official orders. By this time we were completely surrounded. We then, seeing ourselves surrounded, immediately ran into a blacksmith shop. This was a fatal move, for the shop was very open, being made of large logs, one log was cut entirely out on the north side. On the west was a window, on the south was a door and the cracks were all open. We were surrounded by a raging foe who screamed as loud as they could yell every breath, and full determined to have it to say, "I killed a mormon." Each bullet as it passed through these many openings was bound to prove fatal to some of us within. The first man to fall was Simon Cox. He was standing close to my side when he received the fatal blow. He was shot through the kidneys, and all the pain and misery that I ever witnessed a poor soul, in him seemed to excell. It seems as though I could now hear him scream. They came about four o'clock in the afternoon and continued about one hour and a half.

There were eight of our number fled at the start. Such groans of the dying, such struggling in blood, I hope that none that reads this account may ever witness. I remained calm in my feelings without being much excited and realized all that was happening. I thought for a moment that perhaps in the next minute, I may be like these my brethren, struggling in my blood and my spirit take its flight to the spirit world, but soon this thought left me and I possessed an unshaken faith that my life would be spared, although to all natural appearances there was no way for my escape. They were still continuing their firing with an increased rapidity, and closing the circle around us. As they were not meeting much resistance from the few that was left, I looked to the west and I discovered a ruffin who had crawled within about forty steps of the shop and had secured himself behind a large log in the yard of the mill. His head was raised above the log. I went immediately to the west window and stepped up on a block to make myself high enough to shoot. I then saw his gun was to his face and he had sight on me. I immediately dessisted from trying to shoot at his head and dismounted from the block. When I did, another mounted the same block and was immediately shot down. Our number on foot had now decreased to about seven or eight. When Hyrum Abot, the man that had refused to give up his gun, said, "It is useless to stay here any longer—let us leave." I, believing him to be a brave man, thought myself justified in leaving. He started himself, and with him three others. As he left the door of the shop, he was immediately shot through the body, which proved his death. I nursed him in my own house for five weeks and then he was removed to his father's house and died. My brother, Tarlton,[1] was one that started with him He was shot through the shoulder but his wound was not fatal. The names of the other two, I do not remember.

---

[1]Tarleton Lewis was born on May 18, 1805. He was baptized on July 25, 1836, by his brother, Benjamin, whom he buried at Haun's Mill. Tarleton was wounded in the arm in the massacre. He moved to Nauvoo and then to Utah, which he helped colonize. He died in Utah on November 22, 1890, in the Salt Lake Valley.

There were now four on foot besides myself. Benjamin Lewis,[2] Isaac Leeny, Jacot Pots and brother Yokem. I now left the shop alone. I went towards the east where it seemed to be the most strongly guarded. I thought at first I would give into there ranks and surrender myself there prisoner, but, seeing they were shooting and yelling as demons, I felt no mercy would be shown to me. I concluded to try and pass them. I went almost in their midst and then turned down a steep bank of the creek, crossed the creek and ascended a steep bank on the opposite side of the creek in front of Hawn's house. I then passed around the house and went towards the south and crossed the fence which was about two hundred yards from the shop. While crossing the fense, two bullets struck the fence close by my side. They had me in full view for two hundred yards and constantly firing at me. The bullets seemed to be as thick as hailstones when it is hailing fast, and none of them entered my flesh or drew blood, but five holes was shot through my clothes—three in my panteloons and two in my coat. Let me here remark that I did not run one step of the way for I had been confined to my bed for three months with the fever and at that time was just able to walk about and it was about the second or third time I had left the house. The distance from the house was about a quarter of a mile. I proceeded on towards my house, my tongue had lolled out of my mouth like that of a dog, by being overcome with fatigue, and the whole distance was up hill.

A little way from my house, I met my wife who had been in fear for my deliverance, for she had been in hearing distance of the whole scene for she had herd the first guns that had fired. Her first salutation to me was, "Are you hurt? Are you wounded"? I told her I was not hurt and we went with

---

[2]Benjamin Lewis was born on April 22, 1803, and was killed at Haun's Mill.

Aramintee, our only child, and secreted ourselves in a thicket until dark.

I will now return to the fate of the four I left. In the shop, Pots, while leaving, was shot in his legs. He crawled to my house, caught a horse at my door and rode him home. Leany, was severly wounded, having either four bullets in his body or two to pass clear through his body in direct opposition to each other, leaving four wounds in his body and several other severe wounds, but he survived and is now alive in the valley. Yokem, fell just as he crossed the mill dam after crossing the creek on the dam. He was taken in Hawn's house and laid on the floor without attention until next morning. He was shot between the point of his nose and his eye. I picked up the ball next morning where he fell. This was a very large ball and had passed between the point of his nose and eye to the back of his head leaving him senseless on the ground. He was also wounded in the leg, which since has been cut off. He is also alive. Benjamin Lewis, my brother, was found about three hundred yards from the shop by some of the women who had been concealed in the bushes during the fracus. He was yet alive and in his proper senses. I went to him and with the aid of a horse and slide, I got him to my house. He lived a few hours and died. I dug a hole in the ground, wrapped him in a sheet, and with out a coffin, buried him.

Early the next morning I returned to the shop to learn the fate of the rest of my brethren. I first stopped at Hawn's house where I found McBride laying dead in the yard. He was a very old man. He left the shop before me and started to go the same route that I went, but stopping in their ranks, as I first intended to do. When he did, he gave up his gun and himself a prisoner. He was shot with his own gun as I was informed by a sister that was concealed under the bank and witnessed the scene. Jacob Rodgers, then took an old scythe blade and literally gashed his face to pieces. He was taken and laid in the yard where I found him next morning. Merick and Smith was also lying dead in the yard. York and Yokem was in the house at Hawn's but entirely senseless. York soon died, but Yokem lived. Leany, Nights [*probably Knight*] and Hawn were also at Hawn's house and wounded—all of which recovered and none of them had the aid of a physician to probe or prescribe for their wounds.

I then went over to the shop where I found Fuller Cox, Lee Hamm, Richard and two small boys dead on the ground, and several others whose names I do not remember, but whose names has been given in the history of our persecution. The dead numbering in all, eighteen persons, the wounded, fifteen. A few of the brethren who assembled here, with myself, drug those slain to the side of a well which was about twelve feet deep, and tumbled them in, as we had no time to decently bury them, for we knew not how soon they would be upon us again. This was the most heart rending scene that my eyes ever witnessed. The two little boys were not shot accidentally by being in the crowd, but after the men were all done and gone and there was none to resist, they on the outside closed up, and one man discovered these boys concealed under the blacksmith bellows. He deliberately stuck his gun in a crack of the shop and fired at them as they were concealed together. One of their own men reproved him, saying, "It is a d—d shame to shoot such little fellows," he calmly replied, "Little sprouts make big trees," as much as to say, they will make men or Mormons after while, if not killed. They then, presuming all to be dead or dying that remained in the shop, came in the shop and all that was struggling, they shot again, taking deliberate aim to there head and then boasting that they had killed a mormon, and afterwards, to the wives of those that were killed, saying, madam, I am the man that killed your husband.

There were many other acts and circumstances which was equally aggravating that I will not write, for I have no design to enlarge on the tale but to tell the plain facts as they did exist, that after, generations might see and know the things that I have witnessed.

I was then in my 24th year of my age, and my own life was miraculously spared for some unknown reason or purpose to me, but I am willing to bear my testimony to all mankind that God will save and deliver those that exercise an unshaken faith in Him, for I did exercise an unshaken faith in him at that time, and fully believed that I would make my escape and my life be spared. And I then said, "Lord, Thou has delivered me for some purpose and I am willing to fulfill that purpose whenever Thou makes it known unto me, and to all duties that Thou enjoins upon me from this time henceforth and forever."

On the second day after this bloody transaction had taken place, this company of murderers returned to the shop, blowing there bugles, firing their guns and yelling like demons, showing themselves hostile, and as I lived near, I could hear all the proceedings, and myself and Joseph Young went and concealed ourselves in the bush near by, for fear they would come to my house to renew there slaughter.

❦　　❦　　❦

The account of David Lewis that appeared in the Times and Seasons *differs somewhat from the account above, as he enlarges a little more on the story; but it is essentially the same.*[3] *However, he continues with the narration, which is included here.*

[3] David Lewis, "A History, of the Persecution, of the Church of Jesus Christ, of Latter Day Saints in Missouri," *Times and Seasons* 10, no. 1 (August 1840): 147–50. Also available at http://www.centerplace.org/history/ts/vin10.htm

The next day after the massacre a large company of them came back blowing their bugle and firing their guns in an exulting manner. They carried off goods of all description, horses, wagons, and harnesses, stripping the horses and moving wagons of all the goods, furniture and clothing of any value, leaving the widows and orphans to suffer in that inclement season of the years. Cows, hogs, and horses were driven off in droves. They robbed the families of all their beds and bedding, and even took the widow's cloaks; the dead men stripped of their clothing; also another of the persons engaged in this horrid affair was a man by the name of Stephen Bunels, who made his boasts, at public places, that he was the man who killed one of the little boys. This boasting has been made in the presence of the authorities of the state at Richmond, when innocent men were kept in chains for nothing but defending themselves, wives and children from such savages as these.

After this bloody affray was ended, a young man had crept from his hiding place and returned to the shop was sent to Far West to obtain assistance to bury the dead, (a distance of about 20 miles.) The young man arrived within two or three mile of Far West, where he met a company of men: he was asked if he knew where the militia were; he told them he did not know of any. They then told him to face about and go with them, and they would lead him where there were five or six thousands of them. He was then compelled to go to Ray county, and stopped at Samuel McCriston's that night. In the morning they robbed him of a fine fur cap, and ordered him to take off his overcoat, telling him it was too fine for a Mormon to wear. They then concluded to shoot him, and disputed among themselves who should do it. And some hard words and threats were used among themselves who should have the fine horse the young man rode. However they soon quit their dispute and Scarciel Woods, (a Presbyterian Preacher of long standing in Corrilton, the county seal of Corril county.) saddled the young man's horse and rode him about for some time, as if trying him, to see if he would answer his purpose. This was also the same man who took the young man's cap, and his boy wears it now, or did the last information received from that quarter. After being thoroughly satisfied with riding the hores [horse], he dismounted and Samuel McCriston mounted and rode for some time, while Woods was equally engaged in the trial of another horse, which it appeared had been obtained in the same way in which they intended to get this.

McCriston rode off the horse and the young man was taken to Richmond, although he begged to be let loose that he might go and help the widows and children bury the dead at Haun's mill, still he was kept for many days a prisoner at Richmond, in Ray county.

The mobbing party here mentioned, consisted of nine persons, Scarcial Woods, (preacher) Joseph Ewing, (preacher) Jacob Snorden, Wiley Brewer, John Hills (preacher) and four more, their names not mentioned or known. After tormenting the young man all in their power, he was let go, and returned to mourn the loss of friends, without being able or privileged to pay the last debt of honor and respect to his murdered relatives.

A short time after this affair at Haun's mill, Capt. Nehemiah Comstock, the same who commanded a Massacre, with forty or fifty others, took possession of the mill for two or three weeks, and thus cut off all the resources of the widows and orphans who had survived. During this time they lived on the best that the neighborhood could afford, plundering and stealing all the palatable food which had by the industry and prudence of murdered husbands, been laid in store for themselves and families. They burned all the books that they could find, they shot the hogs and cattle, it seemed for pleasure of shooting game, as they did not consume near all they killed.

One day Capt. Comstock with a number of men went to Jacob Fauts, who was at the time laying confined with wounds received in the massacre. They came to question Mr. Fauts, to ascertain where certain of his neighbors were who had escaped the murdering party. Mr. Fauts told them he did not know. I then got up, left the room, but was followed by some of the company, who commanded me not to leave until the captain could see me. The Captain was accordingly called upon and came out to see me; he very gravely and sternly charged me to be gone or on the act of starting on Tuesday evening, this being on Sunday evening. He said I must obey at my peril, or renounce Mormonism. I asked him what I must deny; he said deny that Jo. Smith is a Prophet. As for moving I told him I thought it quite a short notice to get ready to leave the county, and the weather being so cold, and robbed of all our clothing, &c.—I also told him that my wife was quite sick and not able to move so soon, and furthermore the roads are guarded or said to be, so that no Mormon could pass either way without being mobbed. I asked him if I must be driven off by one company, and another lay in wait to murder me as I go. I told him I thought the condition of the treaty was that we could stay until spring: he replied that was the first conclusion, but he had just received new orders from the General, and that was, that all Mormons should be driven out of the state forthwith. I then asked him if the way was not guarded so that I would be in no danger in passing the roads. He said he would give me a pass or ticket which would carry me safely through the state, provided I continued to travel in an eastward course and minded my own business. We soon parted, and on the next day I went to the mill and received my pass which reads as follows. Having the original in my possession I give it verbatim.

> November 13th, 1838
> This is to certify that David Lewis, a Mormon, is permitted to leave and pass through the State of Missouri in an eastward direction unmolested during good behavious [behavior].
> Nehemiah Comstock *Capt. Militia*

The next day Hiram Comstock, the captain's brother, with two or three others, brought a prisoner to me to see, if I knew him; I told them I had seen him, but did not know his name. After questioning me for sometime, they told me to go with them into their camp, and said I might consider myself a prisoner. They kept me until the next day, and set me at liberty charging me to be gone from the state forthwith. I was compelled to comply with these orders at the sacrifice of all I had, and leave the state of Missouri agreeably to the order of the Executive of that state, as thing unprecedented in the history of the world. I was taught to hold sacred the rights of man in my childhood. I was raised in Kentucky, born in 1814, and lived in that state until April, 1837. Such doctrine as taught and prastised (practiced) in Missouri, by the officers of that state was never taught, neither practiced in my native state.

David Lewis

14

The Journal of Margaret Foutz

Although a woman, and alone,
those demons in human shape had to succumb;
for there was a power with me that they knew not of.

M*argaret Foutz was born on December 11, 1801, in Franklin County, Pennsylvania, and married Jacob Foutz on July 22, 1822. After the massacre she and her family moved to Nauvoo. Margaret relates that the men had blackened faces when the massacre first began, as well as in the days that followed.*[1]

❀   ❀   ❀

I am the daughter of David and Mary Munn, and was born December 11th, 1801, in Franklin county, Pa. I was married to Jacob Foutz, July 22d, 1822. In the year 1827 we emigrated to Richland county, Ohio. After living here a few years, an elder by the name of David Evans came into the neighborhood, preaching the gospel of Jesus Christ, commonly called Mormonism. We united ourselves with the church, being baptized by Brother Evans, in the year 1834. Subsequently we took our departure for Missouri, to gather with the saints. We purchased some land, to make a permanent home, on Crooked River, where a small branch of the church was

---

[1]Foutz, Margaret Mann. "Account of Haun's Mill." Subject folder collection, P86, f30, Community of Christ Archives. Also included in Tullidge, *The Women of Mormondom*, 170–74.

organized. David Evans being the president. We enjoyed ourselves exceedingly well, and everything seemed to prosper: but the spirit of persecution soon began to make itself manifest. Falsehoods were circulated about the Mormon population that were settling about that region, and there soon began to be signs of trouble. The brethren, in order to protect their families, organized themselves together.

Threats being made by the mob to destroy a mill belonging to Brother Haun, it was considered best to have a few men continually at the mill to protect it. One day Brother Evans went and had an interview with a Mr. Comstock, said to be the head man of the mob. All things were amicably adjusted. Brother Evans then went to inform the brethren (my husband being among them) that all was well. This was about the middle of the afternoon, when Brother Evans returned from Mr. Comstock's. On a sudden, without any warning whatever, sixty or seventy men, with blackened faces, came riding their horses at full speed. The brethren ran, for protection, into an old blacksmith shop, they being without arms. The mob rode up to the shop, and without any explanation or apparent cause, began a wholesale butchery, by firing round after round through the cracks between the logs of the shop. I was at home with my family of five little children, and could hear the firing. In a moment I knew the mob was upon us. Soon a runner came, telling the women and children to hasten into the timber and secrete themselves, which we did, without taking anything to keep us warm; and had we been fleeing from the scalping knife of the Indian we would not have made greater haste. And as we ran from house to house, forty or fifty women and children. We ran about three miles into the woods, and there huddled together, spreading what few blankets or shawls we chanced to have on the ground for the children; and here we remained until two o'clock the next morning, before we heard anything of the result of the firing at the mill. Who can imagine our feelings during this dreadful suspense? And when the news did come, oh! What terrible news! Fathers, brothers and sons, inhumanly butchered! We now took up the line of march for home. Alas! What a home! Who would we find there? And now, with our minds full of the most fearful forebodings, we retraced those three long, dreary miles. As we were returning I saw a brother, Myers, who had been shot through his body. In that dreadful state he crawled on his hands and knees, about two miles to his home.

After I arrived at my house with my children, I hastily made a fire to warm them, and then started for the mill, about one mile distant. My children would not remain at home, saying, "If father and mother are going to be killed, we want to be with them." It was about seven o'clock in the morning when we arrived at the mill. In the first house I came to there were three dead men. One, a Brother McBride, I was told was a survivor of the Revolution. He was a terrible sight to behold, having been cut and chopped, and horribly mangled, with a corn-cutter.

I hurried on, looking for my husband. I found him in an old house, covered with some rubbish (The mob had taken the bedding and clothing from all the houses near the mill). My husband had been shot in the thigh. I rendered him all the assistance I could, but it was evening before I could get him home. I saw thirteen more dead bodies at the shop, and witnessed the beginning of the burial, which consisted in throwing the bodies into an old, dry well. So great was the fear of the men that the mob would return and kill what few of them there were left, that they threw the bodies in, head first or feet first, as the case might be. When they had thrown in three, my heart sickened, and I turned fainting away.

At the moment of the massacre, my husband and another brother drew some of the dead bodies on themselves, and pretended to be dead also, by so doing saving their lives. While in this situation they heard what the ruffians said after the firing was over. Two little boys, who had not been hit, begged for their lives; but with horrible oaths they put the muzzles of their guns to the children's heads, and blew their brains out.

Oh! What a change one short day had brought! Here were my friends, dead and dying; one in particular asked me to give him relief by taking a hammer and knocking his brains out, so great was his agony. And we knew not what moment our enemies would be upon us again. And all this, not because we had broken any law—on the contrary, it was a part of our religion to keep the laws of the land. In the evening Brother Evans got a team and conveyed my husband to his house, carried him in, and placed him on a bed. I then had to attend him, alone, without any doctor or any one to tell me what to do. Six days afterwards I, with my husband's assistance, extracted the bullet, it being buried deep in the thick part of the thigh, and flattened like a knife. During the first ten days, mobbers, with blackened faces, came every day, cursing and swearing like demons from the pig, and declaring that they would "kill that d—d old Mormon preacher." At times like these, when human nature quailed, I felt the power of God upon me to that degree that I could stand before them fearless; and although a woman, and alone, those demons inhuman shape had to succumb; for there was a power with me that they knew not of. During those days of mobocratic violent I would sometimes hide my husband in the house, and sometimes in the woods, covering him with leaves. And thus was I constantly harassed, until them mob finally left us, with the understanding that we should leave in the spring. About the middle of February we started for Quincy, Ill. Arriving there, we tarried for a short time, and thence moved to Nauvoo.

15

More Interesting Bits and Pieces

*The mob satiated their thirst for blood
[and] retired from their glut of gore.*

S everal short narratives concerning the massacre conclude this *work. The first is the account of Abner Blackburn.[1] Most accounts remark on the mildness of the weather. Blackburn's comments on the use of the well as a grave because of frozen ground does not agree with the assertion by most other testimonies that the well was used for a grave because the victims feared the mob would return and desecrate the bodies. Additionally, there weren't enough uninjured men remaining to dig graves.*

❀   ❀   ❀

Come to a beautiful place called Shoal Creek and began to look around for a suitable place to settle on. [We] had the whole country to select from. The land was rich and wild game [was] in abundance [with] wild strawberies and other kinds of wild fruit. [There were] fish in the streams and bees in the forest with all kinds [of] nuts in the woods. This was truely a paridise on earth.

We had a beautyful place for a home. My parents were verry industrious and they, with the childrens help, soon had plenty of the necessaries of life. By and by other setlers come in to the neighborhood and we had schools for the

---

[1]Bagley, *Frontiersman: Abner Blackburn's Narrative*, 15–17.

children. The grist mill was sixty miles off. A Mr. Haun built a grist mill and saw mill in the settlement. The soil was very productive. I suppose it had not been under cultivation before or since the day of creation. The Mormons taught some verry seditious doctrine [and] my parents objected to it verry much. Their leaders said the Lamanites or Indians would march through the land, slay all the gentiles and the Saints would follow after and geather all the spoil. About this time the Danites were organised, a secrete society to rob the Missourians or gentiles as they called them. The slave holders of Missouri would not submit to have such doctrine taught in their midst and trouble began to brew between the two partyes. The concequence was war.

The Missourians tried to keep the Mormons from voting at the election, which started hostilities. The town of Far West was about twenty five miles from where we lived, which was the head quarters of the Mormons. There was frequent encounters between the two partyes and considerable blood shed. The governer called out the melitia or state troops to settle the quarrel. The Missourians threatened to burn the mills and all the houses of the Saints. All the men turned out to save the mill from being burned. There was some 25 or 30 men guarding the mills.

[It was] in the fall, late, I have forgotten the date. One afternoon two hundred Misourians charged out of the woods and comenced fireing on the mill guard. The party at the mill returned the fire for some time from some shops and out houses, but the odds was against them. The mob shot down about twenty of our party and gave no quarter. A few escape to the woods.

Mr. Eames escaped the massacre and came to our house about dark and said the Missourians were a going to kill all the Mormons on Shoal Creek that night. Every one grabbed

their clothes and ran for safety to the woods. The mob satiated their thirst for blood [and] retired from their glut of gore.

My father was sick with fever and ague, but went to the
mill to assist in burning the dead and caring for the wounded. The ground was frosen so they could not dig graves and
they put eighteen dead bodies in a well.[2] They did not know
but the mob would return and kill them also. Our house was
full of wounded and dessolate families.

❖   ❖   ❖

*The following five accounts are statements sworn before a justice
of the peace. They are all very short. Extra space is inserted where
periods should be; otherwise the statements are copied exactly as
written.*[3]

STATEMENT OF JACOB H. POTTS

I was a sitizen of Mo for ner three years where I selected a
home and purchced the same with my own money in the
Cunty of Caldwell   it being the west half of the south east qr
of Sec 13 T 26 R 56   contained eighty acres   twenty acres of
the same was in astate of cultivation   four acres of it was in
corn   Eight acres in wheat   This being under afree govor-
ment I expected to enjoy Equal rights with other men which
my fore Fathers fought for but in concequence of A decree that
went forth from the governor I was deprived of that privilege
and was forced to dis[pose] of it at a low rate and leave the state
in month of Oct 1838 there was some excitement raised but the

---

[2] In *Frontiersman: Abner Blackburn's Narrative*, editor Will Bagley comments in the
footnote to Blackburn's comment regarding frozen ground as follows (p. 17):
"Blackburn is the first source to explain why the Mormons buried their dead in
the well—or more exactly, a hole dug for a well. Beginning 17 October, eighteen
inches of snow had fallen in thirty-six hours and the weather had been extremely cold for much of the previous two weeks. See LeSueur, *Mormon War*, 116–17."

[3] These excerpts are taken from Johnson, *Mormon Redress Petitions*. Potts and Stiltz
statements, 320–21; Palmer statement, 512; Naper statements, 505–6.

[cause] of it I know not but our lives were threatened in that neighborhood and we met together to council the matter over to now what was best for us to do and the council was adjourned till the next day   Then we met together again durring which time their number of late emigrants came and encamped at the same plac   this being at Hauns Mill   and in the evening about an hour and a half by sun their was a lawless set of bandities   say about two hundred and fifty men headed by Captain Cumstock and Ginings   all on horse back   they came up and commenced fireing on us with out uttering a wor[d] our people began to call for quarters but none was giving   the mob continued their fireing until they had killed and wounded about 30 of our people   16 of them was killed and wounded so they died by ten o'clock the next day   1 boy in four weeks 1 young in 8 weeks   And as far as I know the rest remains alive yet   And amongst the wounded I was one   I received two wounds in my right leg which proved a serious injury to me   I also had a good mare a saddle bridle blanket and halter taken at the same time   Levi Stiltz lost a mare and bridle   Benjamin Lewis was killed   and two horses taken from the widow Isaac Laney severely wounded   William Yokham badly wounded and his horse taken   Jacob Haun was wounded and his critter taken   He was the owener of the mill and land where the fray took place   He was wounded and his critter taken   Charles Jameson and Jacob Foutz was wounded

And a number of other horses was taken from the late emigrants and their was eight of those killed   Two of them was little boys   The names of those that was killed is Benjamin Lewis   John York   Austin Hamer   Simon Cox John Lee   Amos McBride   Mr. Merick and boy   Mr. Smith and boy   Mr. Canada   Hiram Abbot   Josiah Fuller   Mr. Naper   The names of the other four I no not And the mob plundered many things that I have not mentioned   Waggons horses clothing bed clothing & c in testimony whereof I set my hand[.]

Jacob H. Potts

❁   ❁   ❁

STATEMENT OF LEVI STILTZ

I also was a sitize[n] of Mo at the time above mentioned and had entered forty acres of land same manner as is above mentioned   except being wounded   I was at the mill at the same time above mentioned   I had amare saddle and bridle taken   after ward I was taken prisoner and my gun was taken from me   and the same mob passed through the neighborhood painted   plundering what ever they could get their hands on. I can testify that the above ritten is correct.

Levi Stiltz

Levi mentions that the mob was painted, but whether at the time of the massacre or afterward is difficult to ascertain.

The State of Illinois Adams County SS this day (Potts & Stiltz) personally came before me the undersigned justice of the peace within and for the County aforesaid Jacob H. Potts and Levi Stiltz and after being duly sworn deposeth and sayeth that the foregoing statements are facts and that they are correct and true to the best of their belief and farther these deponats sayeth not.

Jacob H. Potts & Levi Stiltz (Sworn to before W. Oglesly, J.P. adams Col, Il. 13 Mar 1840

❁   ❁   ❁

STATEMENT OF ABRAHAM PALMER

Palmer's testimony in a Mormon Redress Petition, sworn to before J. Adams. justice of the peace, Sangamon County, Illinois, November 9, 1839.

Abraham Palmer of Springfield Sangamon County State of Illinois says he is a member of the Church of Latter day Saints commonly called Mormons and that he moved into the State of Missouri in October 1838 and proceeded with his family in a waggon as far as Caldwell County where he arrived two days before the Massacre of the Mormons at Haun's Mill he stopped at a Mr. Walkers about four miles from the said Mill where he remained in his waggon with his family in company with six other waggons of his brethren until after the Massacre. The next day after the aforesaid outrage a company of the mob came to him and brethren and said if you will deny your faith you can live with us in peace but if you will not you must leave the Country forthwith on pain of death for we will exterminate all of you that do not deny your faith men women and children. The above proposition was made by a man who had previously assisted in plundering our waggons he called his name Austin and Styled himself Captain of the Livingston County Spies.

Abraham Palmer

❁   ❁   ❁

STATEMENT OF REUBEN NAPER

Naper's testimony in a Mormon Redress Petition, sworn to before D. H. Wells, Hancock County, Illinois, January 3, 1840.

I Certify that I lived near Hauns Mill about three months. On Tuesday the thirtieth day of October being absent from home at the House of Mr. Walker,   while their a man came up and told us that the mob had come to the Mill and that they had Shown no Quarter, and that they intended to Sweep Shoal Creek. That evening I Started to go to the mill and proceeded some distance   I met Some Families in the Woods who had fled from the Slaughter   We all Slept in the Woods that night without any beds or any thing to Cover us with excepting two women who had brought Each of them a quilt. The next morning I pursued my Journey and went   I got to the Mill   I met my Mother and the rest of the family   I asked them if my Father was dead. They told me to go and look into the Shop   I immediately went to the Shop and Saw Seven men and one boy lying dead amongst whom was my Father who was shot through the head and through the heart. Three more I found lay dead near the Shop and Several more reached Some houses and Soon afterwards died, in all there were Eighteen killed   Sixteen men and two boys.

Reuben Naper

❀   ❀   ❀

STATEMENT OF RUTH NAPER

Ruth Naper was the sister-in-law of Reuben Naper. Hers was also a Mormon Redress Petition, sworn to before D. H. Wells, Hancock County, Illinois, January 3, 1840.

I hereby certify that my husband William Naper and myself lived near Haun's mills about three months previous to the massacre at Haun's which was on the 30th of Octr. A.D. 1838.

The man we lived with who did not belong to the Church told us the week previous to the massacre that the Mormons would all be killed within a month that there wold not be one left a span long in Caldwell Co. In that time. After the massacre was over I went into a certain blacksmith shop where I found my husband dead, he was shot through the breast, there were seven others in the shop dead and dying I did not count those who were dead outside of the shop therefore the whole number killed is unknown to me but I suppose seventeen or eighteen were killed. I judged that there were ~~three~~ at least three hundred of this ~~mob~~ armed force and I heard some of them say there were over four hundred of them. They came upon us on a sudden for they came rushing out of the woods[.] We had a few days previous moved to within a short distance of Haun's mills. After this company had ceased fireing they sent and ~~you~~ ordered me and other women to leave the houses, which we did and then they plundered them of our efforts.

After a few days there came back a large company of armed men and took possession of Haun's Mill and they also crowded into our house and crowded me and my children away from the fire without my consent   they lodged there and one night one of them came to my bed and laid his hand upon me which so frightened me that I made quite a noise and crept over the back side of my children, and he offered no further insult at the time. This company camped in the nieghborhood between one and two weeks to our great inconvenience for they took from the brethren grain, cattle, hogs, bee stands, & C. As free to appearance as though ~~it was~~ they were their own

Ruth Naper

❖   ❖   ❖

An excerpt taken from Pioneering Morgan County *gives an interesting anecdote about an incident in the life of Willard G. Smith.*[4]

Willard G. Smith was a survivor of the Haun's Mill massacre. His father and one brother were killed there, and another brother seriously wounded. He enlisted when a young boy in the Mormon Battalion and marched the entire distance of two thousand miles to California. Soon after arriving, a man came into camp and inquired for Willard

---

[4]Chadwick, *Pioneering Morgan County*, 10.

Smith. On meeting him he told a story something like the following:

"Young man, I am one of the men who shot your father and brothers at Hawn's Mill. I have come all the way to California to forget my troubles, but I cannot forget. Now I want you to shoot me and put an end to my misery." As he spoke he stood up and bared his breast. Mr. Smith answered, "No, I will not soil my hands on you. There is a God in Heaven who will avenge that terrible deed." (Related by Mr. Smith to R. R. Try of Morgan.)

❀   ❀   ❀

Alvin Dyer relates the fate of those who led the forces in the Haun's Mill massacre.[5]

Nearly all who participated in the massacre are now dead, or have moved away, so that their whereabouts, if alive, are not known. Some of the murderers have died in disgrace and shame, haunted by their consciences until their last hours. Others have boasted of their dastardly deeds, until they have been smitten with sickness and misery, in the midst of which they would curse God and die.

The notorious Colonel Wm. O. Jennings who commanded the mob at the massacre, was assassinated at Chilicothe, Livingston County, Missouri, in the evening of January 30th, 1862, by an unknown person, who shot him in the street with a revolver or musket as the colonel was going home after dark. He died the next day in great agony.

Nehemiah Comstock, another lead of the mob who committed the murders, expired years ago in Livingston County, as a good-for-nothing drunkard. His mother was also a drunkard and died a pauper in the midst of misery in a Kentucky poorhouse.

---

[5]Dyer, *The Refiner's Fire*, 252. Dyer gathered this information from the *History of Caldwell and Livingston Counties*, 101.

Epilogue

The site of the Haun's Mill massacre has faded from memory over the years. After the battle, the surviving Mormons moved to Far West as soon as they could, and the promise of a future town in this fertile valley was never realized. Waving cornfields have grown in the surrounding land for years, while bushes filled the banks along Shoal Creek, as if nature conspired to hide the appalling site of this massacre. It is unknown where most of the houses or tents stood on the flat area to the north of the creek, though remnants of houses remain on the hillside. The sites of the mill and blacksmith shop and the location of the well that became a mass grave are only guessed at. Even the exact number of people living there at the time of the killings is unknown. Visitors to the site say that, though the setting is serene and lovely, they can feel a sense of the horror when the wind rustles the corn or disturbs the leaves.

Old-timers in the vicinity say stalks grow higher with perfect corn over the old well. Or grass is thicker over the grave. An old tree, close to the assumed site, refuses to die.

Such stories always have been, and always will be, told and retold with embellishments as the years pass wherever terrible happenings occurred. If these tales were true the old well with its terrible secret would have been easy to find.

In 1888, years after the event, the son of one of the victims, Josiah Fuller, returned to the site after getting directions from a local old-timer named Charles Ross, an early non-

Mormon settler of the area. Both men dug for some time with shovels until they found clay, which they felt was indicative of a former well. This, they reasoned, was the burial site of the victims. On one of the old millstones the victim's son painted the words "In Memory of victims of Haun's Mill Massacre, October 30th, 1838," in crude lettering following the curve of the stone. It was placed where they assumed the burial site to be.

This millstone was lost, but was eventually rediscovered in the deep mud of Shoal Creek. Perhaps the stone was pushed out of the way by a farmer who raised corn in the field. Regardless, the gravesite was lost again.

The people of Breckenridge, Missouri, a town a few miles away, placed the old millstone in their city park some time after 1915. It remains there today, set in cement, to prevent its removal.

But after the millstone was removed from the original site, nothing marked the massacre spot for years. Finally, after more than a century, a program was held at the site of Haun's Mill on July 13, 1941, with local historians and Mormon representatives attending. Mr. Glenn Setzer, a local resident of Kingston, Missouri, provided a commemorative marker for the site. Around 1990 a new wooden marker replaced the deteriorated 1941 marker that had been vandalized and showed signs of decay. Another program was held at Haun's Mill October 30, 1998. Resolutions were offered to improve access and a more adequate interpretive marker for the massacre spot and the common grave was placed near the site of the original mill.

To date no permanent monuments have been built to commemorate the event. Nowhere, to my knowledge, have demands been made for apologies and restitution from the descendants of the perpetrators, even though their names are on record. Nor is there any record of apologies or restitution offered. Despite recent archaeological digs, Haun's

Mill remains today much the same as it was before the settlement developed—only the sound of bird songs, the murmur of the creek, and the wind blowing through the trees.

But its legacy, combined with the other persecutions experienced by the Saints, was deadly. In her book on the 1857 massacre at Mountain Meadows, Juanita Brooks wrote:

> Frictions [in Missouri] developed with the early settlers—frictions aggravated by both sides and inherent in their fundamental differences. . . .
>
> A tragic culmination came in October of 1838, when a band of ruffians fell upon a little settlement at Haun's Mill. Some of the Mormons fled to the woods and took shelter in the brush, but a group hid in an old blacksmith shop, among them a number of children. Of this group, eighteen were killed and a number seriously wounded. When one small boy begged for his life, a mobocrat answered, "Nits make lice," and blew out his brains. That expression was echoed twenty years later on the hillside at Mountain Meadows.[1]

Another historical viewpoint of Haun's Mill comes from historian Alma R. Blair:

> On October 30, 1838, segments of the Missouri militia attacked a settlement of Latter-day Saints at Jacob Haun's mill, located on Shoal Creek in eastern Caldwell County, Missouri. Because the attack was unprovoked in a time of truce, had no specific authorization, and was made by a vastly superior force with unusual brutality, it has come to be known as "The Haun's Mill Massacre." It was one incident in the conflict between the Missourians and the Latter-day Saints that resulted in the LDS expulsion from the state in 1839.
>
> Tensions had been building up ever since the Latter-day Saints began moving into Caldwell and Daviess counties in central Missouri in 1836. From August to October 1838, incidents of overt conflict had grown dramatically. Rumors abounded that the Mormons planned to "despoil" the Missourians and take their land. Specifically, some believed that the Haun's Mill's population

---

[1]Brooks, *The Mountain Meadows Massacre*, 4–5. Brooks later enumerates seventeen dead at Haun's Mill, 57.

threatened to spill over into non-Mormon Livingston County. Outbursts of violence led Governor Lilburn W. Boggs on October 27 to issue an "Extermination Order," demanding that the Latter-day Saints leave the state or be exterminated. It is uncertain whether this order was a catalyst for the attack, but it is clear that both the Latter-day Saints and the Missourians believed that their rights had been violated and their existence threatened.

Thirty to forty LDS families were at Haun's Mill when some 200 to 250 militia from Livingston, Daviess, and Carroll counties, acting under Colonel Thomas Jennings, marched against the village. Assuming that an earlier truce still held, the residents were surprised by the late afternoon attack. Church leader David Evans' call for "quarter" was ignored, and the villagers were forced to flee for safety. The Mormon women and children fled south across a stream into the woods, while the men gathered in the blacksmith shop, but found it a poor place for defense because the Missourians were able to fire through the widely spaced logs directly into the group huddled inside.

Seventeen Latter-day Saints and one friendly non-Mormon were killed. Another thirteen were wounded, including one woman and a seven-year-old boy. No Missouri militiamen were killed, though three were wounded. Certain deaths were particularly offensive to the Saints. Seventy-eight-year-old Thomas McBride surrendered his musket to militiaman Jacob Rogers, who shot him, then hacked his body with a corn knife. William Reynolds discovered ten-year-old Sardius Smith hiding under the bellows and blew the top of the child's head off.

While women cared for the wounded, the men remained in hiding during the night. The dead were thrown into an unfinished well and lightly covered with dirt and straw. A few Missourians returned the next day, took plunder, and warned the remaining Saints to leave Missouri.

The 1838–39 Missouri judicial proceedings investigating the "Mormon War" largely ignored the events at Haun's Mill, but Latter-day Saints wrote numerous, bitter accounts. The Haun's Mill Massacre became embedded in the LDS psyche as an epitome of the cruel persecutions that they had endured.[2]

---

[2]Blair, "Haun's Mill Massacre," http://www.lightplanet.com/mormons/daily/history/1831_1844/hauns_eom.htm, accessed May 2006. See also Blair, "The Haun's Mill Massacre," BYU Studies.

Will Bagley later commented on the massacre: "I don't believe anyone can justify a military attack on civilians. Like the Mountain Meadows Massacre, Haun's Mill was an atrocity. While I've concluded the decent men who committed the massacre at Mountain Meadows did it largely out of misguided religious motivations—what the Missouri militia did was a straight-up criminal atrocity."[3]

The persecutions suffered by the LDS church in Ohio, Missouri, and Illinois left a deep scar on the psyche of the Latter-day Saints. That scar was still fresh in their minds when the Fancher emigrant party, traveling to California through Utah, met their fate at Mountain Meadows in southern Utah in 1857. The brothers and sisters of those slain less than two decades earlier on the banks of Shoal Creek in Missouri were living in southern Utah as the Fancher Party traveled south through the Mormon settlements. Most of the settlers in southern Utah at that time had gone through many of the early persecutions.

Other factors, of course, influenced the Mountain Meadows massacre. The United States Army was marching to Utah to suppress what the federal government viewed as open defiance of its authority over Utah territorial affairs. Word had just reached Utah that their esteemed apostle, Parley P. Pratt, had been stabbed to death in Arkansas, the home state of the doomed Fancher emigrant train. He had been one of the first people to explore southern Utah. But the memory of the Missouri persecutions, and especially the massacre at Haun's Mill, remained fresh in the minds of many Mormons, and a call for vengeance was never far from the tongue.

Alma R. Blair, in his paper on the Haun's Mill massacre, offers his opinion of what caused the massacre:

> They feared these people who were somehow different, who thought and acted in ways that were not their ways. At some

---

[3]Personal correspondence, author files.

point, each of those who marched against the Saints passed from the rational thought that the "Mormons" were also human to the irrational thought that "Mormons" were not truly "people." Their fear had crystallized, leaving them with the capacity to do anything, even kill, to rid themselves of the terror that was silently grinding away. At such a point all defensive or humane acts of the "Enemy" seemed devilish and insincere—all things "We" do are right and necessary. So these several hundred Missourians, made up of husbands, fathers, and sons, marched calmly and righteously through the woods to kill those they "had" to kill.[4]

Mr. Blair tells how the man who had hacked Thomas McBride to death just seconds earlier gently told Olive Ames, hiding with her children under a river bank, that she was safe and would not be harmed. Similar stories often surface in terrible happenings.

Again from Mr. Blair: "Nor were the Saints free from this mob psychology. For some of them fear had also crystallized and their reason had become servant of their emotions. The cause of the Saints' fear-hate reaction is to be found, in part, in the fact they had been pushed too far for too long."

Even those who perpetrated the future persecutions experienced by the Saints in Illinois did not face justice for their crimes against the Mormons. And in many ways this cumulative history finally exploded in the Mountain Meadows massacre in southern Utah on September 11, 1857, when the Mormons had, in turn, become the militia.

September 11—a date that long signified horror to those in any way connected to Mountain Meadows, became a date again etched in history when the Twin Towers fell in New York on that day in 2001. Though almost 150 years separated the two events, the heartbreaking sorrow remains the same, as does the fact that the generations pass, but man's inhumanity to man continues.

---

[4]Blair, "The Haun's Mill Massacre," 65–67.

Bibliography

Note: LDS Archives is short for Family and Church History
Department Archives, The Church of Jesus Christ
of Latter-day Saints, Salt Lake City, Utah.

BOOKS

Allen, James B., and Glen M. Leonard. *The Story of the Latter-day Saints.* Salt Lake City: Deseret Book Company, 1992.

Andrus, Hyrum L., and Helen Mae. *They Knew The Prophet.* Salt Lake City: Bookcraft, 1974.

Arrington, Leonard J., and Bitton, Davis. *The Mormon Experience: A History of the Latter-day Saints.* New York City: Vintage Book, A division of Random House, 1980.

———. *Brigham Young: American Moses.* New York: Alfred A. Knopf, Inc., 1985.

———, and Susan Arrington Madsen. *Sunbonnet Sisters, True Stories of Mormon Woman and Frontier Life.* Salt Lake City: Bookcraft, 1984.

Bagley, Will. *Blood of the Prophets: Brigham Young and the Massacre at Mountain Meadows.* Norman: Univ. of Okla. Press, 2002.

———, ed. *Frontiersman: Abner Blackburn's Narrative.* Salt Lake City: University of Utah Press, 1992.

Bancroft, Hubert H. *History of Utah.* San Francisco: The History Publishers, 1910.

Barrett, Ivan J. *Joseph Smith and the Restoration: A History of the LDS Church to 1846.* Provo, Utah: Brigham Young University Press, 1910.

Baugh, Alexander. *A Call to Arms: The 1838 Mormon Defense of Northern Missouri.* Provo, Utah: BYU Studies, 2000.

Bennett, Richard E. *Mormons at the Missouri: 1846–1842 "And Should We Die..."* Norman: Univ. of Okla. Press, 1946.

Brodie, Fawn. *No Man Knows My History: The Life of Joseph Smith the Mormon Prophet.* New York: Alfred A. Knopf, 1945.

Brooks, Juanita. *John Doyle Lee: Zealot, Pioneer Builder, Scapegoat.* Glendale, Calif.: The Arthur H. Clark Company, 1961.

———. *The Mountain Meadow Massacre*. Stanford, Calif.: Stanford University Press, 1950. Revised edition, Norman: Univ. of Okla. Press, 1962.

Bushman, Claudia. *Mormon Sisters: Women in Early Utah*. Salt Lake City: Olympus Publishing Co., 1976.

Chadwick, Mary. *Pioneering Morgan County*. Morgan County News, 1947.

Carter, Kate B., ed. *Our Pioneer Heritage*. 20 vols. Salt Lake City: Daughters of the Utah Pioneers, 1961–77. Vols. 5 and 19.

Clark, V. Johnson. *Mormon Redress Petitions: docuemtns of the 1833–1838 Missouri Conflict*. Provo and Salt Lake City: Bookcraft, 1992.

Day, Robert B. *They Made Mormon History*. Salt Lake City: Deseret Book Co., 1973.

Dewey, Richard Lloyd. *Porter Rockwell, The Definitive Biography*. New York City: Paramount Books, 1986.

Dyer, Alvin R. *The Refiner's Fire: The Significance of Events Transpiring in Missouri*. Salt Lake City: Deseret Book Company, 1976.

Evans, John Henry. *One Hundred Years of Mormonism: A History of the Church of Jesus Christ of Latterday Saints from 1805–1905*. Salt Lake City: The Deseret News, 1905.

Faulring, Scott H., ed. *An American Prophet's Record: The Diaries and Journals of Joseph Smith*. Salt Lake City: Signature Books in association with Smith Research Associates, 1989.

Fife, Austin and Alta. *Saints of Sage and Saddle: Folklore Among the Mormons*. Salt Lake City: University of Utah Press, 1980.

Garr, Arnold K., Donald Q. Cannon, Richard O. Cowan. *Latter Day Saint History*. Salt Lake City: Deseret Book, 2000.

Godfrey, Kenneth W., Audrey M. Godfrey, and Jill Mulvey Derr. *Women's Voices: An Untold History of The Latter-Day Saints, 1830–1900*. Salt Lake City: Deseret Book Co., 1982.

Hammer, John. "Reminiscence," in Lyman Omer Littlefield, *Reminiscences of Latter-day Saints* (Logan, Utah: The Utah Journal Company, 1888), 66–67.

Hammer, Nancy Jane. "Sketch and Short history of Austin Hammer and wife Nancy Elston," cited in Alvin K. Benson, "The Haun's Mill Massacre: Some Examples of Tragedy and Superior Faith," Arnold Garr and Clark Johnson, eds., *Regional Studies in Latter Day Saint Church History, Missouri* (Provo, Utah: Department of Church History and Doctrine, 1994), 105–17.

Holzapfel, Jeni Brobert, and Richard Neitzel Holzapfel, eds. *A Woman's View, Helen Mar Whitney's Reminiscences of Early Church History*. Provo, Utah: Religious Studies Center, 1997.

Johnson, Clark V., ed. *Mormon Redress Petitions: Documents of the 1833–1838 Missouri Conflict*. Provo: Bookcraft, 1992.

Knight, Nathan Kinsman. "Extracts from a Statement of Nathan K. Knight." In *History of Caldwell and Livingston Counties, Missouri*, 145–58. Reprinted in Joseph Smith III, *The History of the Reorganized Church of Jesus Christ of Latter day Saints.* Independence, Mo: Herald House, 1967, 2: 251–53.

LeSueur, Stephen C. *The 1838 Mormon War in Missouri.* Columbia: University of Missouri Press, 1987.

Littlefield, Lyman Omar. *Reminiscence of Latter Day Saints.* Logan, Utah: The Utah Journal Co., 1888.

Livingston County Centennial Committee. *History of Caldwell and Livingston Counties.* Chillicothe, Mo.: Artcraft Printing Co., 1937.

Ludlow, Daniel H., ed. *Encyclopedia of Mormonism.* 4 vols. New York: Macmillan, 1992.

Lund, Gerald N. *The Work and the Glory.* 9 vols. Salt Lake City: Bookcraft, 1993.

McBride, James. "Autobiography." Microfilm of holograph manuscript, Family and Church History Department Archives, The Church of Jesus Christ of Latter-day Saints, Salt Lake City, Utah. Typescript, Man A483, Utah State Historical Society.

Mulder, William, and Russell A. Mortensen, eds. *Among the Mormons: Historical Accounts by Contemporary Observers.* New York City: Knopf, 1973.

Roberts, B. H. *The Missouri Persecutions.* Salt Lake City: George Q. Cannon & Sons Co., Publishing, 1900.

Schindler, Harold M. *Orrin Porter Rockwell: Man of God, Son of Thunder.* Salt Lake City: University of Utah Press, 1966. 2d., 1983.

Shipp, Richard Cottam, ed. *Champions of Light: True Experiences from the Lives of Latter-day Champions.* Orem, Utah: Randall Book, 1983.

Smith, Joseph, Jr. *History of the Church.* 7 vols. Edited by Brigham H. Roberts. Salt Lake City: Deseret News Press, 1932. Vol. 3.

Smith, Joseph, III. *The History of the Reorganized Church of Jesus Christ of Latter Day Saints.* 8 vols. Independence, Mo.: Herald House, 1896–1976.

Stegner, Wallace. *The Gathering of Zion.* New York City: McGraw-Hill, 1964.

Tullidge, Edward E. *The Women of Mormondom.* New York: 1877. Reprinted, Salt Lake City: 1975.

Turner, J. B. *Mormonism in All Ages: of the Rise, Progress and Causes of Mormonism, and the Biography of its Author and Founder, Joseph Smith, Jr.* New York: Platt & Petters, 1842.

Whitney, Orson. *History of Utah.* Vols. 1–4. Salt Lake City: G. Q. Cannon & Sons, 1892–1904.

Wilcox, Pearl. *The Latter Day Saints on the Missouri Frontier.* Independence, Mo., 1972.

DOCUMENTS AND ARTICLES

"A Rare Account of The Haun's Mill Massacre: The Reminiscence of Willard Gilbert Smith." *MMFF (Missoui Mormon Fountier Association) Newsletter* 13 (Summer/Fall 1998). Also at http://www.jwha.info/mmff/mletr098.htm.

Blair, Alma R. "The Haun's Mill Massacre." *BYU Studies* 13 (Autumn 1972): 62–67. Also found at http://www.farwesthistory.com/ hmblair.htm.

"Far West Public Square." http://www.jwha.info/mmff/fwsq.htm.

James McBride. *Autobiography of James McBride.* Typescript, L. Tom Perry Special Collections Library, BYU Provo, Utah.

Johnson, Clark V. "Missouri Persecurtions: The Petition of Isaac Leany." *BYU Studies* 23 (Winter 1983): 94–103.

"Joseph Young's Affidavit of the Massacre at Haun's Mill." *BYU Studies* 38 (1999): 188–202.

"The Haun's Mill Massacre and the Extermination Order of Missouri Governor Lilburn W. Boggs." *Religious Studies Center Newsletter* 12 (September 1997): 1–5.

NEWSPAPERS

Fayette, Missouri, *Boon's Lick Democrat* 1841. Document Containing the Correspondence, Orders &c, in Relation to the Disturbances with the Mormons.

Grunder, Rick. "Newspapers for Sale in the Electric Bookshop." http://www.rickgrunder.com/newspapersforsale.htm.

[Lamoni, Iowa] *Herald* 1897, Reorganized Church of Jesus Christ of Latter-day Saints.

McMinnville, Ore., *News Register*, March 8, 2005.

New York. *New Yorker, A Weekly Journal of Literature, Politics, Statistics and General Intelligence.* Volume 1838–39.

New York *American*, June 27, 1839.

Reorganized Church of Jesus Christ of Latter Day Saints, *Saints' Herald.* 42: 676, 45: 452.

Standard Atlas of Caldwell County, Missouri: Chicago Geo. A. Ogle & Co. 1817.

Times and Seasons 1 (1840): 145–50. See http://www.centerplace.org/history/ts/v1n10.htm.

JOURNALS—INTERNET

Blair, Alma R. "Haun's Mill Massacre." http://www.lightplanet.com/mormons/daily/history/1831_1844/hauns_eom.htm.

Eames, Ellis. "Haun's Mill Massacre." http://ww.richardsonfamily.homestead.com/Ellis.html.

"Frequently Asked Questions." http://ldsfaq.byu.edu/view.asp?q=57.

Index

150, 175; Mormon settlement at, 19, 85–86, 166; surrender to militia, 37, 80, 82

Fontz, Jacob. *See* Foutz, Jacob

Forrest, Edwin, 8

Foutz, Jacob, 45, 54, 115, 131, 147, 159, 161, 168

Foutz, Margaret, 161–164

Freedom of religion, government protection of, 16

Frontier violence, Haun's Mill massacre as, 8–11, 179; prevalence of, 7; rule of law and, 23

Fuller, Josiah, 36, 44, 54, 114, 131, 147, 155, 168, 175

Gallatin, Mo., 22

Gee, William, 31–32

Gentiles (non-Mormons), 28, 166

Greene, John P., 90–92

Green, Hervey, 117

Hammer, Austin, 11, 93–101, 131, 147, 155, 168

Hammer, Austin (son of Austin), 99

Hammer, Jacob, 147

Hammer, John (father of Austin), 93

Hammer, John (son of Austin), 9–11, 93, 99

Hammer, Josiah, 99

Hammer, Julian, 99

Hammer, Nancy (daughter of Austin), 99

Hammer, Nancy Elston (wife of Austin), 93

Hammer, Nancy York (mother of Austin), 93

Hammer, Rebecca, 99

Harmer, Augustine, 36, 44, 54, 114

Haun, Jacob, 19, 21–22, 29, 45, 54, 106, 118, 131, 150, 168

Haun's Mill, Battle of Crooked River and, 23, 87; building of, 103; burial location at, 175–176; burial of the dead from, 36–37, 46–47, 53–54, 59, 64–65, 96, 106–107, 114, 121–122, 147, 155, 163, 168; as criminal atrocity, 179; as forgotten act of violence, 8–9, 175–177; Missouri investigation of, 178; survivor's stories of, 9–11; vapor like a pillar of blood at, 10, 93, 96–97

Haun's Mill massacre, anonymous account of, 39–47; Ashby account of, 83–84; author historical account of, 20–21; Bancroft account of, 15; Blackburn account of, 165–167; Blair historical account of, 177–178; county history accounts of, 79–81; Ellis Eames account of, 141–148; Olive Eames account of, 137–141; Foutz account of, 161–164; Greene account of, 90–92; Hammer account of, 93–101; Holcombe account of, 27–38; Knight account of, 109–115; George Laney account of, 133–135; Isaac Laney early account of, 127–131; Isaac Laney later account of, 131–313; Lewis account of, 149–160; James McBride account of, 117–125; Myers account of, 103–107; Reuben Naper account of, 170–171; Ruth Naper account of, 171–172; *New Yorker* (magazine) account of, 82–83; Palmer account of, 169–170; Potts